Copyright 2019 by Patricia Simon

***MY FIGHT CLUB WITHIN***
Copyright © 2019 by Patricia Simon

All Rights Reserved. This book may not be reproduced in whole or in part, in any form or by any means, mechanically or electrically, including photocopying, recording, or by any information storage, printing, retrieval known systems or future invented without prior written permission by the author.

This book is my memoir. It is simply about my step-by-step journey to how I have learned to accept, and take care of, my full self. It is how I choose to live my life and how it works for me. This book is for entertainment only, and neither the author nor the publisher can guarantee your success nor provide medical advice. Also, the information in this book, cannot supplant professional advice from a physician or other doctor. If you feel you need emotional or medical support, please seek the proper medical personnel.

**Project and Line Editor:** Patricia Simon
**Contributing Editor:** Liz
**Cover Design:** Dominic
**Illustrator:** Elena R. Brown

**Library of Congress Cataloging-in-Publication Data**

Simon, Patricia.

*My Fight Club Within*/Patricia Simon

p. cm.

**ISBN: 978-0-578-77179-3**

1. Self-help   2. Memoir

# In Praise of *My Fight Club Within*

"Patricia, thanks for your inspirational writings and being 'real.' Your awareness is key and spot on! The truth is hard to swallow sometimes but sharing with others is healing! It has been such a blessing to call you a friend. Best wishes on your continued journey we call life!" ~**Regina E.**

"Dear Patricia, *My Fight Club Within* was so relatable. The honesty and transparency in your story are truly authentic. I could feel your vulnerability turn to strength as the words on every page formed a perfect picture in my mind as if I went on this journey with you. I'm excited to see where life brings you. My new friend, you are unstoppable! Sincerely with appreciation." ~**Trish B.**

"*My Fight Club Within* is an eye-opening read that really equips you with the tools to fight your battles to first love yourself and then be able to love others. This is a great guide to leading your life and other lives to personal freedom!" ~**Patrick O.**

"*My Fight Club Within* is a very realistic book with struggles that everyone deals with. In this book, you will find the realism of life and the different options to take to live it to the fullest. It's up to you to actually implement these words of wisdom in your life and truly live in complete freedom." ~**Dawson E.**

"*My Fight Club Within* is soulfully written and embraces life's experiences with such relatable experiences. Patricia's ability to come to self-realization of her past, turning it into an amazing journey, brought to light some of my personal inner controversies as well. I applaud her bravery and look forward to my personal journey to come." ~**Brooke W.**

"Patricia Simon's metaphor of the boxing ring is inspired. Through her examples and struggles we can all gain strength to follow our own paths and gain confidence." ~**Christine H.G.**

"*My Fight Club Within* was inspiring as I am on my own personal journey to self-love and acceptance. Let your inner spirit guide you through, and you shall prevail." ~**Charlotte H.**

"A splashy poolside tell-all blended perfectly with the hard-earned lessons of a seasoned and thriving survivor; Patricia Ann will win your heart and make you a better person in the process. A wild ride, a warm hug, an honest and crystal-clear view through the eyes of a true-hearted beauty. Just try to put it down!" ~**Elizabeth A.**

"What a privilege to be given the rare opportunity to see our world through the eyes of someone like Patricia Simon. With her vividly captured thoughts and unique writing style, she is gifted with the ability to virtually paint the pictures of her mind inside your head. I believe she has miraculously turned a challenge into a triumph with her book, *My Fight Club Within*." ~**Mark G.**

# TABLE OF CONTENTS

Acknowledgments ................................................................. i
Introduction ..................................................................... viii
1. Love ........................................................................... 1
2. Joy ............................................................................ 11
3. Peace ......................................................................... 21
4. Patience ..................................................................... 54
5. Kindness .................................................................... 65
6. Goodness ................................................................... 74
7. Faithfulness ............................................................... 85
8. Gentleness ................................................................. 97
9. Self-Control .............................................................. 116
10. Catastrophizing ........................................................ 141
11. Secrets .................................................................... 158
12. Death ...................................................................... 173
13. Spiritual Warfare ..................................................... 182
14. Soul Awakening ...................................................... 184
15. Forgiveness and Healing .......................................... 194
16. Removing My Mask ................................................ 202
17. Change ................................................................... 218
Epilogue ........................................................................ 224

# Acknowledgments

Now that I've completed *My Fight Club Within*, I think back with much love, appreciation, and gratitude on the incredible people who have surrounded me from the very beginning through the final steps of my book.

These awesome and beautiful people have generously dedicated their time, skills, amazing talents, and pure loving kindness in the beautiful creation of this book, *My Fight Club Within*.

The time capsule…

I must begin with beautiful Liz, my contributing editor, yoga coach, videographer, closest and dearest friend, and the first real person I met here in paradise.

She was teaching yoga on the beach when I first saw her, and I was drawn to her inner radiance of beauty.

One morning after the end of taking her yoga class, I simply blurted, "Would you like to edit my book?" And, without hesitation, she replied, "Yes!"

Liz is the foundational cornerstone of *My Fight Club Within*, without her, there would be no book. She is hands down the perfect fit, the only person who gets me, who can read me, who knows how to make that wonderful and magical connection with you, my dear reader.

For me, having dyslexia, meant that writing this book has become the greatest challenge of my life because I see things in pictures, not words. So, it's like a roll of film continually going through my brain; thus, imagine Liz's dedication and intuition in editing my book.

One very important piece of subject matter is that I know my friend and copyeditor, Liz, has been patiently waiting for me to hit on.

You must understand sweet Liz and how amazing and incredibly talented she is in her role and position of being my personal one-on-one Crazy Whisperer. Seriously, there is no other human being on this face of the earth that knows just what to whisper, and exactly what I needed to hear, do, or write in *My Fight Club Within*.

Her work here will go down in history as the only one capable of reining in my all-over-the-place and off-the-wall outrageously deep, intense, and bizarre writings.

Let it be noted that this could only be accomplished as she rocks in making all my crazy-ass stories fit perfectly into place in every paragraph and onto every page.

Gratitude is the word for you, Liz. I'm still in awe of how I knew as it clearly must have been my SPIRIT that led me to you. You didn't even know me for more than five seconds when I so boldly asked you if you would like to edit my book.

Without hesitation, you replied, "Yes."

I was in shock when you said, yes, scurrying off and running all the way home, trying to write this whole dang book in one week, just in case you would change your mind. I know I wore Darla out with my excitement of having you as my editor.

Gratitude was your word again this morning in class when you softly spoke it out in front of your twenty-some yoga students plus me in the back humming, "Om," in my SPIRIT for and with you, my beautiful friend.

You inspire me, Liz, and I want to be just like you, but of course, not the Crazy Whisperer role because I have way too many dysfunctional friends; I would have non-stop laryngitis.

I am so grateful that you said yes, Liz, and I speak out for the people connecting here on these pages in *My Fight Club Within* that they too feel your sweet presence of love poured out in these words.

*My Fight Club Within* would not exist if it wasn't for Liz. The universe, along with myself, my family and friends will forever be grateful for all your hard work.

Then came Jim McDonell, my Business Coach, and his beautiful wife, Monique, my very first best friends I met in Mexico during my travels in 2017.

One day I was on the phone with Monique discussing my book and how I need to build a website, and that's when she offered up her hubby Jim.

So now there's Jim and Liz in my world. Keep in mind that in my head I see the big picture as being perfect and there's no problem too big to solve. Being dyslexic, I envision the end as being perfect in all the details and aspects of life. I must because there's no room for anything else to fit in my brain!

In my writings, with accepting myself and making that radical change of getting real and raw, Liz and Jim were the very first to experience my authentic self.

The editing task made Liz and I more and more connected in our friendship, and Jim does his best in managing and coaching this dyslexic me.

Then one morning I spoke with one of my oldest and dearest friends, Dez. We had not spoken in a long while, and she asked,

"How are you really doing?"

At this point, I'm so overwhelmed with myself in my writing of *My Fight Club Within*, that I don't even want to talk about myself. All I want to talk about is how this story of launching a book is unfolding; again, I see the big, positive, magical picture.

Dez exclaims, "You need my son, Dominic, to build your website. He's brilliant, young, and hungry to help make your story reach millions of people. I promise you he will be cheap for you."

I said, "Okay, give him my information."

Dez replies, "I told him. You know, he's a good kid and will do you well."

She sent him this text, "Pat, my maid of honor in my wedding looking for a simple, cheap, cheap website to promote her book okay. Call her."

Before noon, there was a three-way call with me, Dominic, and Jim. I sat back quietly, listening to the conversation between two men excited about *My Fight Club Within*, and I was ecstatic to hear and see the big and beautiful picture of all my ideas coming to life.

An hour later, after I received this text from Jim, "Hi Patricia. I think you struck gold with Dominic!" The next day Dominic had my book cover downloaded and website built!

It was almost springtime, and I was out with my friend, Melinda, for dinner at a roof-top restaurant, watching the sunset.

Sitting next to me was my latest awesome new friend, Trish. She was in town for a convention with her work, and it was her birthday. We're having a great conversation as we spoke about my book and what I'm writing.

It's kind of funny when I think about how, when I am asked what my book is about, I never answer except to explain that it's very deep and it's about everything. Then I talk about the challenges I'm having in publishing it. Trish and I became instant friends even though she lives quite a distance away.

I feel so close to her and value her opinion so much that I ended up sending some details on my book and share that what I need is an illustrator.

A couple of weeks later, I received some sketches from her, and she asks, "Is this what you're trying to capture?" She explained that her daughter Elena sketched these drawings to capture what I wanted. She then goes on to say how Elena's mentors are quite famous, and she is interested in doing this for her school project.

I write back to Trish right away and say that I appreciate this hard work, but I don't think I can afford Elena. I then ask how much she would charge. To my wonder, in her text reply, she said, "There's no cost to you. It's about connections with strong women, opportunity, and gaining experience."

Precious beautiful Elena fits into a perfect place as the Illustrator for *My Fight Club Within*.

In a minute, I was off for the weekend to hang tight with my girls Trish and Elena. Trish did my hair, dressed me in Elena's dress and shoes and took my picture of my "marriage to myself" for the first chapter, Love. Wow!

I want to give special thanks to my illustrator, Elena R. Brown, a talented art student who captured my spirit through her creative interpretations. Elena's passion for digital and visual illustration shows through in her beautiful works of art.

After finishing the book, Liz and I recorded an interview video for the website. It was brilliant! But sadly, we found out later that the rain had drowned out our words so we could barely be heard.

Soon after, I was having dinner with a new man in my life, Eric, a physicist doctor. He is a very busy person, developing a team and setting up seven clinics in the area and making arrangements with people all over the world.

At this point, I hadn't shared with him too much about my book, but I told him about my recent video. I couldn't believe this man when he told me he has the software to tune out the rain and he would take care of it for me, even with all the things he was juggling!! Hurray!

What I love best is capturing the moments of the makings and the people behind the scenes of *My Fight Club Within*. I can't begin to explain how bad my tummy hurts from gut-wrenching laughing with Dominic in Colorado saying how it's hard for him to understand Eric with his British accent, and how he can converse on all the technical details of fixing and implementing my video on my website.

My fabulous and awesome friends, Darla, Iris, Faith, Marla, Brooke, Monique, Dez, Adine, Regina, Holly, and Susy, I'm just so glad and ecstatic we step out and experience all the spectacular, fantastic, and wonderful good times we share.

I know I sometimes refer to y'all as being my dysfunctional friends, with me as the pied piper, the silliest and goofiest of all. However, how cool is it to be accepted by one another as our true selves. Words written here cannot express my deepest gratitude for you my best girlfriends, especially in all the times, you have been there for me in *My* (Fright) *Fight Club Within*. I love you.

Back in my early business years, my beautiful friend and mentor, Rita Davenport, who by example taught me how to balance through commitment in being assertive with internal discipline in making all my hard work pay off.

I am forever grateful for her in providing all the excellent Management Training Seminars I attended with the Worlds' Greatest Speakers – Og Mandino, Tony Robbins, and Jack Canfield, to name a few. To all my success teammates all over the world. What a privilege it was to train, learn, and grow with you!

To the Hoffman teachers and classmates, my most prized peeps that are my extended family and supporting my authenticity in me being me, Patricia Ann.

To Verl and Earl Brede, the real Notebook couple that through their example of long lives have demonstrated the purest example of love and marriage.

To my four sets of parents beginning with my biological set – Fred and Vera, Howard and Sue, Carl and Mary, Whitey and Lillian, I thank you.

To their offspring, my village of childhood playmates, neighbors next door and across the street: Shelley, Rozzie, Ruth, Robbie, Tony, Ricky, Glen, Jerry, Diane, Donna, Gail, Debbie, Harvey, Pat, Eddie, Maryann, Russell, Wayne, I thank you too.

To the quirky one somewhere out there that God specifically created me for, thank you.

It wasn't all fun in games when I was totally alone inside my ring, but I'm a believer! As weak and raw as I felt inside my restless soul, I was relentlessly digging out the big old deeply planted root of guilt and shame. Layer upon layer, as I continued to peel, I was exposing my deepest and darkest kept secrets. Did I feel like quitting? Yes! But through my faith and beliefs, I prayed and meditated daily for God's wisdom as He guided me through with His word.

Hebrews 13:5 (AMP) says, "I will not in any way fail you nor give you up nor leave you without support. I will not in any degree leave you helpless nor forsake nor let you down" Patricia Ann.

I give all praise, glory and honor to the Most High and Yeshua, which live inside the temple of my body, and to the Holy Spirit that fabulously lights my path.

Last but not least of all, with enormous love, to all my amazingly beautiful children Tatum, Patrick, and John, and grandchildren; Dawson, Ella, Kinsley, John, and Luke (the baby boy on the way). Thank you in loving me through my journey from the very start in all my words written throughout *My Fight Club Within*.

This book is for you!

# Introduction

Imagine inside, within our core, a black boxing ring. There are four corners. There inside sits an immature CHILD in corner one, and an ADULT ego in corner two, jittery, tensed-up BODY in corner three, and charged-up SPIRIT in corner four. Your SPIRIT-light patiently waits to unleash the endless power of true freedom.

Welcome to my book, *My Fight Club Within*. I want also to let you know that I have written the companion workbook, which enhances the information I present. *This is How I Fight My Battles Workbook* is available on Amazon, Barnes & Noble, IngramSpark, and other online resources.

My hope in sharing *My Fight Club Within* is that together we may experience growth in a deeper sense, realizing that we are so much more than what we see as a reflection of ourselves on the outside. In fact, our image is so different from the very same image of ourselves that others see. We are such beautiful and unique, one-of-a-kind beings with an awesomely divine spirit that beams with a power that can only be driven with your permission. Your spirit will never input force on you against your will. Spirit can only proceed by your total surrender in love.

When I speak of my unique CHILD within, I speak of my unique child within as a vestige reminder of my early years. I full-heartedly believe that through sharing my experiences from history to present, I will demonstrate many challenges I face daily, especially with having a learning disability that my dad couldn't accept and forced me to keep hidden.

This sweet child of mine may merely be acting out in ways that she never had the chance to actually experience, reveling in the opportunity to feel her own feelings now. I recall quite clearly the example of sadness. It's a Sunday evening, and my mom is dropping off a much younger version of me after a long, fun day. Little Patty goes inside with teary eyes, already missing mom. Daddy says flatly, "Stop your crying; you'll see her again next Sunday."

Many similar instances over the years have ingrained deeply in me a path for running away from my inner child, which is timeless in me. This path leads to peaceful light out, radiating pure love and joy. I was told to avoid sadness and cover up my tears.

In corner two, ADULT ego awaits its turn to push in and take over as boss, pointing its finger exclaiming, "I know what's going to happen here next. Mark my words as I can clearly see what the outcome will be!"

As an ADULT, when led by my SPIRIT, I exude patience, kindness, and goodness.

The BODY, flesh, which contains my faithful heart, gentle soul and feet that ground me into the earth, when they are walking in self-control; not-so-patiently waiting in corner three, comes out swinging, swallowing its convulsions to be dealt with later.

In corner four, stands the light of SPIRIT. The SPIRIT is my guiding light that leads and directs only when I am present. SPIRIT is LIGHT that instantly drowns out the darkness and turns my bad and ugly into goodness. The SPIRIT peacefully waits for the opportunity to radiate its effortless power of resolve, not to overcome the others, but to uplift and embrace the fullness of each member of the fight.

Yep, that's me in my personal war-zone battleground with and within myself. My CHILD is continually complaining about her same old silly past ouchies. My ADULT ego is ablaze with concern, worried solely with self-preservation. My BODY is all wound up in a tizzy, hyperventilating into a paper bag. As my true SPIRIT awaits my cry to relinquish my all.

How do I get to my safe place out of the ring and out of being stuck and alone in those dark corners? How can I assist my SPIRIT with moving from the oppressed and tiny, smoky amber hue to beaming out in full radiance?

My SPIRIT will only lead me when I relinquish my control. It is only in the present moment when I let go (of my ADULT ego, my CHILD and BODY) that I become equally yoked with my total being. I must get out of my ego head, release worries about the past or future, and be in the present moment so my SPIRIT can lead me. My heart is connected, and at one with the entire universe. In that present moment, my tiny spark ignites into a flame of purity and clarity. I step out to be my true self, in love, joy, peace, patience, kindness, goodness, faithfulness, gentleness, and self-control.

Only when I finally extended my inner self out to the universe, am I able to receive, embrace, and engage, experiencing that oh-so-wonderfully fabulous moment of true oneness. Residing within that alignment, I can recognize all the love that is, and has always been, right there within my reach.

My transformation began taking form with these three simple steps:

Step 1. Awareness – if I feel

Step 2. Action – I can heal

Step 3. Allow – and be real

When I think of transformation, I think of one of my favorite quotes from my cousin, Gail. I'd been experiencing a difficult time in my life, and the choices that led me there had been my own. "Patsy, have you eaten enough turds yet?

When is enough, enough?" she asked me.

It was then when I opened my eyes and became aware that the fight was within me, nobody else was there in my four corners. Just me, catastrophizing in fear, filling with numbing feelings, experiencing that on-and-off lump in my throat and a deep ache in my belly. Just me, myself, and I, duking it out on myself.

It was in that ah-ha moment when a switch went off inside me. I'd been taking abuse in my life and felt that I was the only one, but I realized that I am not alone – everybody suffers. In fact, at this very moment, millions of people are suffering deeply within. I became aware, imbued with the understanding that it is natural to have these feelings. It was my very own glorious moment when I was able to intentionally shift my direction to freedom. I realized that sometimes I may have a bad day and can easily assume the role of presiding Grand Duchess over my very own little pity party. After all, I know I am not perfect. I'm a human being, and I'm going to make mistakes, but I don't have to live, breathe, and revel in my mistakes, staying stuck and repeating the cycle over and over and over again. Yes, it was then when I had my fill and had eaten my last turd.

When I am breathing into all my being, living in my present moment of truth, embodying my authentic self, I am truly able to love myself. Acting from that place of love, I can finally get out of the corner seats of my CHILDish behavior, ADULT intellect, and anxious

BODY. With a whole lot of forgiving, giving, and receiving a group hug within, and allowing my Spirit to take control, I am free to transcend the entire situation. It's all about becoming one as a team, offering my Spirit the opening to lead me in blossoming into a brilliant, emotionally, and intellectually mature human being. Only then am I able to love me so that you can love me, and I can love you – connection baby! Are you getting the picture?

I've been a daughter, a friend, a wife, a mother, and a lover. And now, I'm myself.

It's been a worthy journey, and I've finally found out who I am inside.

It wasn't easy; sometimes, it seemed I was fighting myself. Soon, I'll share my story of *My Fight Club Within*. It's the story of the battles I survived to get to know me. Welcome to *My Fight Club Within*.

The first rule in My Fight Club is – there are no f*cking rules.

The second rule in My Fight Club is – THERE ARE NO f*cking rules!

*This is how I fight my battles.*

# 1. Love

*"If I love myself, I love you. If I love you; I love myself." ~Rumi*

Love. They say it's what makes the world go around, the common denominator between us that connects and ties us all together in this cosmic universe. It's also noted that it's impossible to love another if you don't love yourself first.

Hate is a place where I will admit to having dwelled much too often. Even amidst such chaos, I had no clue at the time that I was in a prison of my own making. I was embroiled in, and far too preoccupied with, operating from the wounds of my past. At the time, this was what I knew, and it felt like my comfort/safe zone.

Leaning into my transformation, I decided to honor this significant change with a deeply personal ritual. First comes love, then comes marriage. Yes, I took the big step, but with myself. In fact, my wedding reception is still present now within me. I committed to love, honor, and take care of myself till death do I part. This is my never-ending love story, my soul-written vows from within. There is no beginning and no end. There is only now.

**Figure 1: WEDDING DAY**

## *Falling in Love*

Falling in love with someone is one thing, but to fall in love with yourself is a whole different story. Sharing this hard-earned lesson is my purpose in writing this book entitled *My Fight Club Within*.

You may be asking yourself what does *My Fight Club Within* have to do with falling in love with one's self? So how did I come up with that title?

Let's begin by talking about love and how we go about falling in love with another person.

I think back to my first love. His name was Brian. The moment our eyes met, I felt a sudden warmth of energy surging through my being, in and out. It was as though an arrow, shot out from the bow of Cupid himself, had lifted me up and off my feet.

I was a junior in high school. One day, walking home with my best friend, she talked me into taking a shortcut through the woods to a neighborhood to visit her cousin. I was walking alongside her, on a beautiful sunlit path, impatiently questioning, "How much farther? Who is your cousin? Where does she live?"

Just as my friend pointed her finger, I noticed up ahead stood a tall, handsome guy in a white T-shirt and jeans working under the hood of his car. It was Brian. Right away, I said to my friend, "Oh my God, I'm in love! He's the one I'm going to marry."

My friend said, "Oh, I know him; let me introduce you to him."

I was like a butterfly dancing on air as we walked over to him. He apologized for being covered in grease from working on his car, and he wiped his hands. Then, he reached for mine.

I literally fell head over heels in love for the first time. We would go on to have many beautiful and romantic dates with many long picnics in the fields of flowers by the waterfalls at Rivers Run. We would go out and spend hours picking, preparing, and eating fresh crab from the bay nearby. Taking long drives down crooked and winding roads lead to a few fondly remembered sessions of making out on Lovers Hill.

Brian always kept his car immaculate. One night, I remember that we were going to a party with live music. We were walking hand-in-hand, very close together when suddenly I fell into a manhole. I was drenched and covered in mud from head to toe.

He was the ultimate gentleman, so sweet in getting quite muddy himself from carrying me and putting me into his immaculate car. All the while, he was comforting and assuring me that it was okay and that he was merely happy that I didn't get hurt. I was his dirty girl.

He took me home, and I made sure he was gone when I took off my clothes on the front porch. There was no way I could walk into my mom's spotless home in my muddy clothes.

I'll never forget the startled look on her face as I stood before her in my bra and panties as she screamed at me, "Patsy, where are your clothes?"

### *Love is Everything*

Love is everything; from flowers and butterflies to picking crabs and muddy manholes. The key is to build a relationship with someone that is based and founded on self-love. Brian had selflove because if he didn't, he would've most likely been a real dick to me when I muddied his clean ride.

We all know that there's no age to love; it's timeless. When I was studying the topic of love back in college, I learned that there are three types of love:

1. **Demanding Love** – Everybody is born with this type of love. We cry to get our diapers changed and cry to get fed.

2. **Conditional Love** – You love me first, and then I will love you back.

3. **Agape Love** – Love with no conditions.

I know without a doubt that if I love and accept myself unconditionally, my partner will respond in the same loving manner towards me. So, if he doesn't, well, let's say he will no longer be my partner because he doesn't love himself.

### *Tiki Bar Versus Castle*

Life and love on the beach took on a whole new meaning for me.

In October 2018, I went from traveling the world with my six-foot-three Aussie boyfriend, with him holding my hand every step of the way, to being by myself, getting a sweet little one-bedroom place here in paradise, surrounded by views of the water.

I'd gotten out of a relationship, moved to a new city and knew absolutely no one. I was alone and on my own for the first time in my life. I didn't like it one bit.

### *Everything Reminded Me of Him*

I love to walk, especially by the water, so I started a habit of walking the beach daily, from one end to the other. I like to walk fast, keeping a fairly rapid pace. Usually, a very satisfying experience, something had changed. I noticed it was so different for me walking alone now. I was longing for friendship.

At times I'd stop and turn towards some of the live music I'd hear in the distance. Resolute in rooting into my new territory, my lonesome self would plow through the sand and up towards the source of the sound.

### *The Tiki Bar*

I'd squeeze myself in amongst all the happy couples that were there either vacationing, honeymooning or on a fun work-related trip. I was envious as I observed how perfectly love fit snuggled in between all these beautiful people.

I would next gather up my courage by initiating some friendly conversation by first introducing myself. Then, further breaking the ice by cheerfully asking friendly questions such as

"Where are you from?" Followed by "How many more joyful days do you have until your vacation is over?"

I would then share my experiences of my big move here and how I lived within walking distance. More often than not, I'd get the same response back, which would usually sound something like, "Do you know how lucky you are? Wow, you get to experience and be here all the time. How cool is that? I am so jealous of you."

Just beneath the surface of this conversation, my real feelings rise.

My ADULT head is feeling sorry for myself, and my CHILD is feeling abandoned as my lonely BODY sits next to strangers. I am feeling isolated and all alone in paradise. I couldn't be further away from this carved-palm stool.

My relationship hadn't worked out, and yet, I found myself missing my Aussie boyfriend and reminiscing on all our spectacular adventures and connections with other strangers.

What I missed the most was being in love.

I would leave the tiki bar soon after and go home to my sweet new place and cry my eyes out. The next day would be like Groundhog Day. I'd be walking like a crazy New Yorker, eagerly in search of making new friends. And, once again, I'd be faced with the same scenario, happy couples but with different faces. Dinner alone would be even worse.

One of the saddest scenes from one of my favorite movies, *Sex in the City*, is Mr. Big sitting at the bar alone eating his steak dinner amongst happy lovers on New Year's Eve.

This cycle and sadness went on for days, then weeks, until one beautiful day I slowed down my pace to stop directly in front of the most beautiful Castle. The Castle wasn't what this place was really called, but in my heart, I'll always call it the Castle.

I rinsed the sand off my feet, strolled by the pool and found a seat at the beachfront bar.

Up ahead was a beautiful woman standing in Tree Pose, with the longest full braid of hair falling down her side. She was facing me and a group of relaxed and content people who were practicing yoga gazing into the sea.

### *I Found My Happy Place, and I Knew I Belonged There*

In the Iconic Castle, I had a plan.

The next day I went all out, above and beyond in fixing myself up. I fixed my hair, flat ironing it, and applied makeup for the first time in months. I slipped into my cutest dress and strutted back to the Castle in my Jimmy Choo shoes.

Stepping inside the historic, iconic Castle is a true immersion into the most wonderful and spectacular atmosphere. I was mesmerized and captivated by its beauty and charm. Brilliant details dress the entry, walls, halls, and ceilings. Overhead float the most breathtaking chandeliers. A baby grand piano played softly in the background, and the air was filled with the smell of exotic tropical florals.

I was on top of the world. I felt like Elle Woods (played by Reese Witherspoon) in the movie *Legally Blonde 2*, when she journeys to Washington, D.C. to have her say about animal rights; but she is ignored by every politician she encounters. Elle eventually enlists the help of a sympathetic congresswoman who helps her get the foot in the door. Eventually, Elle gets to have her say.

I felt like Elle in that I could do anything. I was captivated by its beauty, and I was in love.

I knew that I knew that I knew that this is where I needed to be, to work and spend my time. I had never felt more confident as I did that day when I walked into the fitness club. My spark was back, and my groove was on.

I was about to connect and make my very first friend. I'll call her Sara.

It was as if she already knew me and immediately picked up on many of my best talents, even some that I had forgotten I had. She knew I would be a perfect fit in the Castle. We connected and bonded that day. Her desire for me to be there was just as strong as mine. Sara would talk to her boss and create a job specifically tailored just for me.

I made a friend. I got the job and found myself gleefully employed shortly after that.

### *I am Learning from My Mistakes and the Mistakes of Others*

You may beg to differ with me but hear me out. I will provide you many personal examples as you read on, through these pages.

When I was living in my world of guilt and shame for many years, because of my background and not wanting to be a failure, I was in year twenty-three of my marriage. I found myself staying married to somebody just for the mere purpose of making myself look good and appear happy to others. Most of my energy was spent working hard at measuring up to the high standards, conditions, and rules that were dictated to and planted in me throughout childhood. I was taught growing up to perform, being everyone's Patsy, or their Miss Goody Two-Shoes. My existence of relying on what other people thought I needed was more important than knowing my own identity.

My mission and top priorities were God first, family and friends second, and my career third.

I kept my marriage vows, being faithful, respectful, and supportive in all my husband's future education and career decisions. I encouraged him to attain all his goals, many of which centered on making more and more money, buying bigger houses with bigger yards and bigger swimming pools.

We uprooted and moved our three kids while each in their high school graduation year. My husband had twelve career changes throughout our marriage, climbing the ladder with me in the background cheering him on and at the same time trying to appease my sad and unhappy kids.

I would not only have the perfect five-unit family, but we would live in the best neighborhood with the nicest houses and in the best school district. We would all appear to have it all in being beautiful on the outside.

However, where was the love for myself? My love?

If you were to see the person I was ten years ago, before I got my wakeup call in January 2009, it would be a totally different person than I am now. I'm still discovering me in this very moment, as I reflect on all the things with which I covered myself, allowing in stuff that would continuously suck the life out of me.

The beginning of my life-changing transformation was walking away and leaving all those things behind. I can say I have traveled just as Julia Roberts did in one of my favorite movies, *Eat Pray Love*. She played a woman who thought she had everything she wanted until her perfect marriage fell apart. She then went on a trip to find herself through Italy, India, and Bali.

So today, as I share through my beam of light, ever shining from the ring of my fight club, I have nothing but love from within. Yes, indeed, I have my precious CHILD, my brilliant ADULT, and my healthy BODY in harmony, with my SPIRIT leading the way.

### *My Personal Love Anecdote*

I opened this very book, *My Fight Club Within*, with the first chapter on love, sharing the sacredness of my marriage to myself.

And so, I will continue keeping my promise to be and remain true to myself.

With my SPIRIT leading me upward in love… Forever and ever…

My love chapter one is never-ending…

*This is how I fight my battles.*

# 2. Joy

*"It is in the nature of things that joy arises in a person free from remorse." ~Buddha*

Joy leaps out as I'm practicing yoga at the beach on a beautiful sunshiny day in January 2019, breathing in the fresh, salty air as the waves splash up on the sand.

My mind is totally in alignment with my heart when breathing into every cell of my body. I am grinning from ear to ear in total bliss with my spirit dancing. Leading from within, I feel complete and one with the other people as we are dancing on clouds after a beautiful class. Suddenly, my cell phone buzzes, and I answer with a happy "Hello?" Much to my surprise, I received devastating news.

Sorrow rolls into shock and awakens my inner being with a gut-jerk reaction inside my knotted throat as my belly begins to ache. Again, the seats are taken in each corner of the boxing ring within my being. Dark clouds were now blanketing over those beautiful rays of sunshine while the soft waves are now crashing thunder within.

My SPIRIT is timeless. However, when my all-time-consuming ADULT ego, fearful CHILD, and turbulent BODY react to bad news, look out! The sh*t is about to hit the fan.

Here I go into the next round of suffering. Damn, it hurts, and it hurts badly. I choose to face it and not run away. I remember that everybody suffers, and millions are suffering as well at this very moment. I'm not alone, and I am only human. I am going to switch on my light, group hug, cry if I must, maybe get on my knees on the side of my bed, and beat my pillows for five minutes. I will deal and fully feel this sorrow of heartbreak. However, I will not stay here; I will allow these emotions to be as the clouds that are constantly shifting. I choose to shift with them and not to remain stuck. This will be a short round, as I pray immediately for guidance for my SPIRIT to lead me back to my joy. Do you want to know what happened? This is what I wrote to family and friends.

*Dear Friends and Family,*

*Last Wednesday, I posted a personal post/pic update of me picking out my dress in preparation for chapter one, "Love", of my soon to be published book, My Fight Club Within.*

*In chapter two, "Joy", I receive a devastating phone call (1/10/2019), but I choose not to reveal or put the subject matter of the news of the call in my book.*

*1/4/2019 had blood work drawn for working as a volunteer at a Children's Hospital. The call that I received went like this, "Patricia, we have your lab results in, and you have tested positive for Tuberculosis. We suggest you come in for a chest x-ray to make sure that it's not active, maybe Monday, this was on a Thursday when I received a call. As I was running up to land from the Beach, and at the same time saying, could you please repeat that again? As she did. My reply was, hell no; I will be there at the hospital in ten minutes for this chest x-ray. As I did show up and my chest was clear, and they* stated, well it's inactive, so you are good to go as far as being able to work with the children."

Well, at that point, I was in shock because I had recently traveled all over the world.

Next step for me that very same day was to immediately find a doctor, who is now my good friend Jennifer. She explained how she could start me up on three months of antibiotics, and I would be fine. Of course, I was being a difficult patient as I absolutely hate taking antibiotics because they make me sick!

So, she wrote up my order to get Quantferon /Future (On Hold) requested Collection date 1/14 and said just go and get it done. Of course, I procrastinated.

Until Friday 6/7 2:45 p.m., I have blood drawn to find out if I have inactive tuberculosis so I can begin three to six-month treatments with antibiotics. I finally got the courage up to face that debilitating news.

Right after 3:00 p.m., I'm on the road for a three and a half-hour drive to meet illustrator Elena and work on my book. Saturday, the next day was when my photoshoot was taken by Trish, Elena's mom, which really took my mind totally off what I might soon have to endure.

Monday, as Jennifer my doc calls me with the most beautiful news, Patricia, your test on 1/4/2019 results was a False Positive. 6/7/2019 results are Negative. You do not have Tuberculosis.

So, my chapter two Joy is quite lovely after all as I now share my most joyful news with you.

I just really want to be totally transparent with all of you that know and are closest to me.

*I will continue to share some of my fondest, sad, and silly behind-the-scenes adventures here on my page, so that when you are reading MFCW, you will relate (as my editor had exclaimed, I was wondering what that meant with that phone call of devastating news!)*

*Remember also that soon I will be sending out personal invitations to you as I will be giving out free copies of my book and other fun gifts to my Friends and Family in using these personal Wednesday notes as extra treasures... Until then, keep smiling.*

*With enormous love and excitement!*

*xoxo Mom, Nana, Patricia*

*This is how I fight my battles.*

### *Single Versus Taken*

I am at my best when I am in a loving and healthy relationship. I will confess that traveling with my Aussie boyfriend around the world was the happiest time of my life. From the start, it was instant chemistry between the Aussie and me. On our first date in February 2017, we met on a Saturday at five o'clock and did nothing but talk for the first two hours in the lobby of the restaurant. We continued to carry on non-stop talking throughout dinner. He chuckled in saying he is now homeless. I shared my plan of moving to Paradise. By nine o'clock, we were off to listen and dance to live music. Our date ended at two in the morning. We both agreed it was the best first date ever!

We both shared in having a mutual friend Becky. He knew her as his former neighbor and realtor, who recently sold his house. Becky is one of my closest and best friends and has been for over thirty years. We had called her in Southern California in the first ten minutes of meeting each other in the lobby. I'll never forget her exact words of "Oh my God, Pat, I can't believe you two found each other." We met in Texas, and he is from Australia.

She continued, "There are no two people in this entire world that go together as well and that are more perfect for each other than you two, but don't you dare hurt him, don't you break his heart."

I now understand why she said that because he had just gotten out of a long relationship three and a half months prior. It was a bit hard for me in understanding his accent, and I thought I heard three and a half years. It would be nine months later, while in Mexico, that I discovered this fact.

### *Mahalo, Hawaii*

Our second date was on the following Monday, where we discussed and made plans for our third date, which would take place in Lanikai, Hawaii. He had invited himself to come out to Hawaii and join me, and without hesitation on my part, I said, "Sure." I already had plans in motion to spend two weeks with my son and his wife and a week meeting up with a guy whom I had been dating back in Dallas. He owned a beautiful home in Kauai, quite near my upcoming destination.

I then phoned my kids explaining that there had been a change in plans, that I had met somebody and he's coming out to join us at the end of my three weeks. I decided not to see the other guy. That was the beginning of our relationship of travels in paradise, to the most beautiful places on the face of the earth. We spent eight solid days enthralled in each other's company. There was no sex, just sleeping together, enjoying being wrapped up and snuggling tightly in each other's arms. I've never slept as peacefully well with anybody as I have with him.

Our first night, he had gone to the bathroom, and as he was coming back, I turned and rolled over, jerking up my elbow. Albeit accidental, it was such a forceful blow that I heard a crack, giving him a black eye. I was devastated, but he took it as a man that would become my hero.

### *Greenest St Paddy's Day Ever*

The next day was St. Patrick's Day; we attended a fabulous party with my kids dressed from head to toe in green. He held steady, undaunted by his sad, pitiful, black, and blue eye. Our third date took place under the full moon in Lanikai, Hawaii. We spent the entire day hiking up a lush mountaintop, then back down and around babbling brooks connecting to the pool of water that we would find the most picture-perfect place to honor. Then we took lots and lots of pictures while gazing back up to the magnificent waterfall cascading down upon us.

### *Swimming, Hiking, Kayaking, Oh My*

Then our road trips and love for music joyfully continued here in the USA, with stops in New Orleans, Eureka Springs, Nashville, Memphis, and Austin, Texas.

We never grew tired from our countless hours of meaningful conversation in planning our next adventures.

We'd dance our nights away in perfect rhythm under the starry sky. Then, we'd wake up and do it all over again the next day.

Life was so much better together.

Our globetrotting spanned a great many countries. We started in Bali and continued to Ubud, Badung, Gianjar, Indonesia, Bangkok, Thailand, Hanoi, Vietnam, Osaka, Kyoto, Japan, Chetumal, Bacalar, Quintana Roo, San Perri, Caye Caulker, San Ignacio, Belize, Roatan, Honduras, Tulum, La Paz, the Sea of Cortez, Mexico, Gold Coast, Brisbane, Sydney, and Melbourne, Australia. I have included some photos from these trips at the end of Chapter 3, starting with Figure 2.

## *Bali: The Bunnies, Monkeys, and Toads, Oh My!*

Love and joy were in the air, finding me on the back of a motorcycle with my arms wrapped tightly around my lover.

I was dressed in my fancy little black dress and in platform shoes to stand tall next to my slim, handsome Aussie boyfriend who was also shining brightly in his Sunday best.

He was my rock of protection, creating a space of safety around me that I valued every step of the way. He would take great care to physically secure me, always strategically placing and strapping my helmet over my long head of hair.

Driving a motorcycle on the crowded and narrow-lane alleys and streets in Ubud is serious business. You've got to know what you're doing. I always felt safe and sound weaving in and out of the sea of motorcycles.

It was an extraordinary night, and we're on our way to enjoy the best mojitos in town. We spotted two great seats facing the street; we love to people watch. We ordered our drinks and some food when all a sudden, my belly began to cramp up.

## *Bali Belly. Oh No!*

The lady's bathroom was nowhere near us. The restaurant was crowded with tables full of people dining. At this point, relief was only to be found after walking through a large courtyard, past the towering five-tiered fountain, down a wide, tiled staircase, and finally through another dining room full of people. Ladies room. Yeah!

I stopped counting after eight trips.

My Aussie boyfriend and I agreed it was time to go. We got on the bike with our helmets secure. He said to tap him on the shoulder if I needed him to pull over. With that, we were on our way.

Things only proceeded to get worse for me. I don't know if it was the fumes from the other bikes or the volcano ash in the air, but right away I felt the pangs of nauseating convulsions. We were going over a bridge when I tapped him on the shoulder. I felt my belly and dinner rising again, and I couldn't hold it in any longer.

He went over the bridge and didn't stop. Instead, he pulled in front of the poshest and popular five-star restaurant, complete with servants at the doorstep. A seemingly endless pool of beautiful people dressed in tuxedos and evening gowns were heading inside to dine.

We parked, hopped off quickly, and I still couldn't manage to get my helmet off in time. As my dear Aussie boyfriend pulled it off my head, puke shot out everywhere. He was so sweet and kind, running inside to get an ice bucket and water to clean my face and wash the wretched output off the sidewalk.

I was the person the people watched that evening as I wore my little black dress and my high platform shoes returning forth what last little bit was no longer acceptable to my stomach.

Thank God, I had my hair back in a ponytail.

Yes, I had the worst case of Bali belly. My boyfriend thought I needed another run to the bathroom in a restaurant. All I could see happening at that point was me hanging my head over that bridge.

That was the beginning of the romance of really getting to know each other. This is the reason why we went on to experience so many more countries full of joyful adventures together – we shared the good, the bad, and the ugly. The vulnerability of it all had opened a door between us.

## *My Personal Joy Anecdote*

My SPIRIT will only lead me when I give up my control. It is only in the present moment when I let go of my ADULT ego, my CHILD and BODY, that I become equally yoked with my total being; myself, with my heart genuinely connected as one to the universe. In that present moment, the spark of purity ignites a flame that engulfs my existence; I am on FIRE! I'm stepping out to be my true self, in love, joy, peace, patience, kindness, goodness, faithfulness, gentleness, and self-control. Only when I finally extended my inner self out to the universe was I able to receive, embrace, and engage, experiencing that oh so wonderfully fabulous moment and that love that is right there within my reach. My transformation began taking form with these three simple steps:

Step 1. Awareness – if I feel

Step 2. Action – I can heal

Step 3. Allow – and be real

## *Back in Paradise*

Settling into my new life after the Aussie, with my new friend and job in the Castle in 2018, I felt a sense of purpose. I actively attended and participated in every opportunity, and class my new friend was teaching or attending. I even went so far as to attend a wake with her and her husband, dispersing even then, great efforts to meet people. I signed up to begin the process of volunteering at the Children's Hospital, which has proven with every moment to be my most important job.

Thanksgiving was approaching, and I was slowly but surely coming out of my funk. My neighbors threw a huge potluck dinner, and we all gathered together for our Friendsgiving Feast.

The Castle was throwing a Christmas Party, and I was invited. Of course, I had an invitation for two, but it was just me, myself, and I. I dreaded being alone for the holidays. Even though I had a ticket to go home to be with my family and friends, something was guiding me to stay put. I was still lonely and sad, yet at the same time, I was beginning to get to know me, more so than ever. At last, I was acknowledging realizing the presence of my powerful SPIRIT, my source of the endless supply of all the love and joy that is alive within me. Oh, baby, she's got it!

My boyfriend, family, and friends can never take the place of my unique, one-of-a-kind beautiful heart and soul. After all, I am already taken! Authentic joy took root in those days of discovering myself. Daily honoring of my SPIRIT connection deepens the source, enriching my journey from an immovable place, deep within.

*This is how I fight my battles.*

# 3. Peace

*"Those who are free of resentful thoughts surely find peace." ~Buddha*

Peace readily arrives and is present in those joyful moments of being in love. In loving myself first, I can love you and others. On my daily walks, in any venue, as long as there's nature, trees, or water, is where and when I experience peacefulness; in those magnificent moments of full presence. I can be alone, with my lover, a friend, or even a pet.

I have found that my personal peace from within is what is most important for me. I do cherish my newly found peacefulness in every single breath I take.

My commitment to keeping my peace is to remain calm and exercise my breathing throughout the day.

Sometimes at night, I'll wake up as if in a panic with a choppy and shallow breath. I'll then slowly begin reciting a prayer, focusing on breathing slowly in and out on each word, allowing my soul to be nourished and flourish. It usually works as I tend to peacefully go back to sleep with my SPIRIT gently caressing my nighttime existence.

During the day, in practicing my breathing, I may have to exert more effort and energy when the choppy, shallow breath sneaks in. My CHILD loves swimming against the current while my ADULT intellect demands that my BODY/belly continue the practice of exercising deep and full breaths in and out. It is when I stop all the things that I feel must be done with great immediacy and do nothing except breathe, my happy SPIRIT veils over me with its crown of glorious peace.

Anxiety can come over me without warning, the very moment I start worrying and thinking about my future or dwelling on my past. Fear can set in quickly, stealing my peace with worries such as, "Will I have enough money? Why didn't I tell him how I was feeling?"

Grrr… here comes that telltale clearing of the throat and then down to my unsettled tummy. All the while, my SPIRIT is yearning for a group hug and the opportunity to illuminate the way out of this silly nonsense.

I will go back into my peaceful state of walking in love and light; for it is impossible to feel anxiety when I am fully present. I will be thankful and live in this moment, experiencing peace and joy within. I then plant a big, big smile on my face and at the same time, try to frown to test myself.

Frowning impossible, I have succeeded.

*This is how I fight my battles.*

## The Lonely Clusterfuck Fest

I feel that the number one cause of breakups in relationships is not loving yourself. When there is no peace within, there is only an endless empty void continually and consistently flowing in and out with the same old issues into our bottomless pit. Not only do we lose ourselves and all self-respect in the ongoing process, but we push away our most important best friend and lover.

When one partner begins to be exceedingly influenced by the opinions of others, friends, and family about how they should and need to live their life, your relationship will surely die.

It's hard enough when you're trying to sort out your true feelings between you and your partner. However, when you go against your true self by allowing others in, guided now by their opinions, your needs and the needs of your romance fly out the window.

Fear and anxiety begin to take hold, replacing the reality of yourself/your partner with second-guessing your own decisions. Even from the start of the relationship, did you allow your family and friends to erode your precious clarity with their own choices regarding whom they think you need to love?

All too frequently, I've found myself bombarded with others parroting an array of concerns. What is his nationality, and from what country does your partner come? How does your partner present himself and dress? Is your relationship age-appropriate? What are his ideals, beliefs in politics, and views on religion? Is your mate educated and living up to all their standards as to what you need? Where must you and your mate cohabit? What is your mate's income? What career/business do you need to have and is it best suited for you?

Concerns may arise within your circle of loved ones and their attempts to define the path you should take may engulf you; however, there is only one person who can answer and must decide.

I followed my Aussie boyfriend around the world and put him first in everything, and I lost myself. I'm venting for my peace.

However, there is only one person that can answer and must decide, and that person is me.

No longer will I act on what other people think or care or say for me. Only my SPIRIT will I lean on with providing me my true peace from within.

*This is how I fight my battles.*

### Should-haves, Could-haves, and Would-haves

When one dwells in the lonely land of all your past should-haves, could-haves, and would-haves, it is quite easy to become lost; especially if hopelessly living in and for somebody else's shoulds, coulds, and woulds, brought about your should-haves, could-haves, and would-haves. Guilt-ridden feelings quickly fill the once-clear skies. "Am I destined to be alone?

Surely, I don't deserve happiness. This must be my punishment."

By now, your lover is long gone. Nobody wants to or should have to compete with their mate's family and friends dictating and controlling their life. Nobody wants to witness their love fade away into shame and guilt by sacrificing themselves to others. It's downright exasperating to see them spreading themselves thin like peanut butter, trying to please everyone only to exist on the crust of others.

Left alone now and trying to make sense of what the hell just happened, you see your happy family and friends experiencing and living out their own lives. They are in love with whom they choose to love. They live happily together where they want to live while creating and making all their own important life decisions. There is no peace within when we exist in the universe solely for others. This has been a big life-changer for me. Taking care of myself is my number one priority.

### Because I See Pictures Only

My emotions range widely in writing and searching out of words to fit and line up here on these pages for you, the reader. They are on and off, up and down, hot, and cold, slow, and fast, and all over the place. I feel as if I'm on a roller coaster experiencing the quickest ride of my life, and there is no safety bar to hold me back.

I'm fervently driven with capturing your interest and warm regards to my words written; I desire a genuine heart-to-heart connection with you. I work day and night in writing *My Fight Club Within*. Every free moment I have in between my jobs at the Castle and Children's Hospital are dedicated to putting my words and genuine experiences down on paper.

Every evening I make my nightly call to a very close and dear friend of mine, Darla, to review my latest chapter. I then await her thoughts. She is upfront with me and never sugar coats the truth. After listening to her kind, warm and encouraging opinion, I once replied with a chuckle, saying, "It's hard to believe, but I guess I can honestly say that I'm a writer now."

She was so upset with me for laughing at myself. She scolded me and said that I should be proud of myself and my hard work as a writer. So, she had every right to be upset with my disregard in minimizing myself.

### *I am a Writer*

I am a writer. Like the words of another good friend of mine, Faith, set in, I am further filled with that acceptance. She spoke out with the joy of absolutely loving my book, exclaiming, "My God, Patricia, I had no idea that you had such a gift in writing. I related so well and was picturing myself within the four corners of my own fight club within. I say this with all honesty for the world will relate. You are writing a best-seller. Girl, please don't be offended but your book fucking rocks."

## *My Personal Peace Anecdote*

When we seek approval and demand it from others without giving the proper appreciation in valuing ourselves, frustration is imminent as we will never feel and experience our worthiness from within.

Step 1. Awareness – if I feel

Step 2. Action – I can heal

Step 3. Allow – and be real

## *My Pathway*

I feel as if my feet have walked a million miles and then some through every street, path, and trail you can imagine.

From in between swells, waves of the ocean alongside mountains in Hawaii, to cliff climbing on the edge of the sea in Belize and in the Sea of Cortez, hiking pillbox trails straight up steep mountains in Hawaii, from dark alleys in Japan to narrow dirt roads in Honduras, kayaking to the islands, strolling in the Queen's garden in Buckingham to petting the kangaroos in the outback, snorkeling in the oceans to speeding fast and furious on a Quad with hungry pit bulls on our tails, walking through and crossing into the intense traffic of Vietnam with only a hair's space between body, car and me, I have traveled many roads. Then, as my Aussie boyfriend and I make it safely back up onto the curb and into our hotel room falling into each other's arms and knowing how we made it into that peaceful, loving place of birds chirping in through the window and sunlight beaming on rays of light, I realized how lucky I was.

## *Homeless*

While traveling throughout the world to all these exotic places, my Aussie boyfriend loved introducing us to people as being homeless. It didn't bother me being homeless as I felt just the opposite. I knew that I had total ownership of my cool car and belongings, all being safely stored. I felt the world as being my present home, and I was experiencing pure blissful joy in my awesome adventures in just being. I was living my beautiful plan and path of freedom being connected as one to the universe.

High-speed walking, yoga, watching, and hearing all of nature keeps me well and grounded in peace. I surrender in honoring my SPIRIT to lead my every step.

I am deeply thankful for all my beautiful old and new friendships that encourage me daily with loving kindness and a feeling of peace that warms my soul.

*This is how I fight my battles.*

## MY TRAVELS

I see the world in pictures without words.

Figure 2: THE JOURNEYS BEGIN

**Figure 3: HAWAII**

Figure 4: HAWAII

**Figure 5: HAWAII**

Figure 6: NEW ORLEANS

**Figure 7: EUREKA SPRINGS**

**Figure 8: GALVESTON**

**Figure 9: SOUTHERN CALIFORNIA**

# MY FIGHT CLUB WITHIN

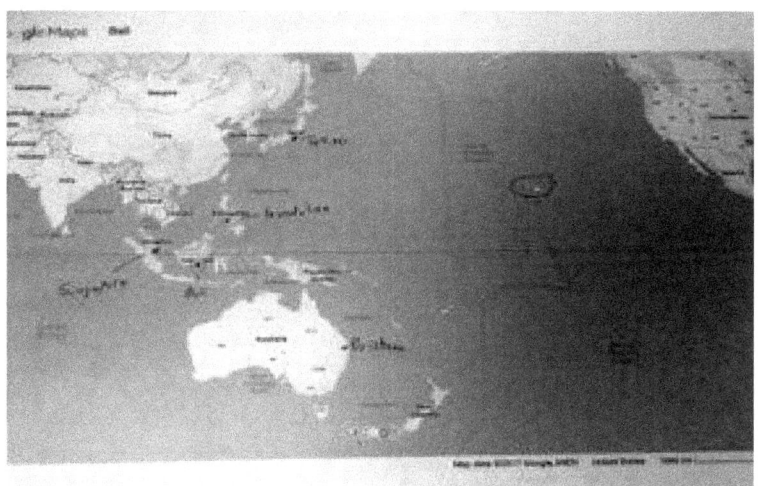

**Figure 10: BALI**

**Figure 11: BANGKOK**

**Figure 12: HANOI**

**Figure 13: HANOI**

Figure 14: HANOI

**Figure 15: DA NANG**

**Figure 16: JAPAN**

**Figure 17: OSAKA**

**Figure 18: MEXICO**

Figure 19: BELIZE

**Figure 20: AUSTRALIA**

**Figure 21: AUSTRALIA**

Figure 22: AUSTRALIA

**Figure 23: AUSTRALIA**

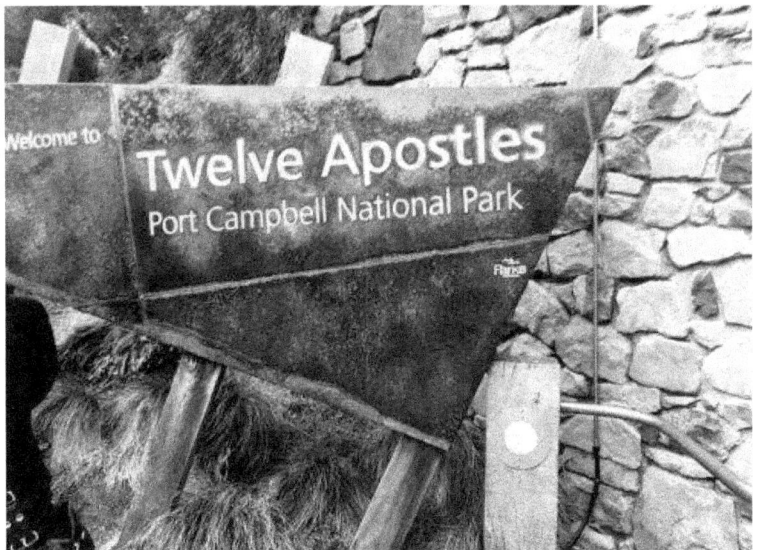

**Figure 24: AUSTRALIA**

**Figure 25: AUSTRALIA**

**Figure 26: AUSTRALIA**

## 4. Patience

*"Endurance is one of the most difficult disciplines, but it is to the one who endures that the final victory comes." ~Buddha*

Patience, first with myself, is imperative as I feel this is my weakest area that I must face daily. I feel the heavy desire to have all my needs met promptly and addressed ASAP.

I have just taken up meditation and find that practicing first thing to begin my day makes a huge difference. Patience is a practice that must be honored moment by moment, led by my SPIRIT. It is especially important to cultivate and remain focused on deep breathing. My regular flow (or mantra) is "Let breath in… let breath go. Let Go!"

Frustration laid heavy on my shoulders shortly after moving to the beach and after many attempts of working hard at creating my dreams and making them come true. My friends and family from whom I moved far away thought, at first, I was crazy to leave. All I kept imagining was my atmosphere where the sea, earth, and sky connect, surrounded by beauty with my toes in the sand, watching sweet nature jumping up out of the water under a sky full of breathtaking sunrises and sunsets.

Sadly, within the first couple of days of living by the sea, I was taken with the panic and frustration of being without all my city conveniences such as Whole Foods, Sprouts, Discount Tires, sushi restaurants, and even friends in my new area.

I knew no one. I was so impatient and frustrated that I wasn't enjoying being present in living and experiencing my dream. So, my friends and family went from telling me how crazy I was to "How brave are you to make such a big move! Do you realize that there are very few people that will ever do such a thing in a lifetime? And look at you girl, you are doing it! Living your dream! You are in paradise."

### *True Connection*

My love connection is family and friends – my people encouraging me with love and reinforcing my true self; reminding me of my dream, my new life. However, I'm embarrassed to admit that I stayed stuck in this round of total chaos and frustrations of thinking I made a mistake moving to paradise. Hmmm, but wait, there is absolutely nothing wrong with feeling my emotions and experiencing them. After all, it's only natural to be afraid, and it's perfectly okay for me to cry, and cry and cry. Which is why I am diligent and continuing with writing this book that I began almost two years ago.

I am working this out as I write. I am adapting to the beach life. I am learning to chill. Even if I am a crybaby, I am in cleansing with my tears, and nothing is holding me back. It's my wedding party, and I'll cry if I want to. I will continue to learn to be my authentic self.

*This is how I fight my battles.*

### *Being Married*

The happiest and proudest days of my life was in the beginning in giving birth to my three beautiful babies in the 1980s. By my side was a responsible hardworking husband, providing us with our first new four-bedroom home when I was eight months pregnant with the youngest of the babies. We'd worked hard together as a team in taking care of our babies and at the same time maintaining our home inside and out.

I love gardening and designing landscaping with getting my hands deep in the dirt. I'd start with my spray paint can in hand drawing the perfect outline for where my husband needed to dig for my beds to be planted. Nine months pregnant, I'd be bent over on my knees planting my masterpiece and still got guys honking driving past and loved turning around, so they'd see my big round belly. Oh, what fun to see their look of disappointment.

Slowly my life became less important as my children grew. My focus was strictly on them – Husband going to school at night getting his Master's degree, the kids and I cheering him on at his baseball games and me encouraging him with his career. We both agreed that I should stay at home and raise our kids. This had extended my focus so not only was I cheering on my husband, but I was also cheering on my three kids with all their education, music, and sports.

Seems like my life before the above is kind of like my life now. Seems like my life has come full circle like it was before.

I had gone through a divorce, a young single mom with my three-year-old little girl. We loaded up the car, and we moved to Southern California to start a new life. We stayed with my uncle at first and then got our little place close to the beach. I had a great job, and my boss, Becky, became my best friend.

My sweet little girl and I were happy. Life was good.

I met my second husband, and we got married. Becky was my maid of honor and my baby our flower girl.

Into our second year of marriage, we moved far away. Problems arose early in our marriage that caused me to leave my husband. I was five months pregnant and traveling with my son and daughter on a flight back to California to stay with Becky. All four of us snuggled into her king-size bed.

What a true friend. She has such a beautiful and patient kind heart to take in a pregnant woman with two babies.

I spoke with a therapist, and I knew I made the right decision to leave, but my husband would not let us go.

A couple of years later, I went back alone to visit my friend, Becky. I wasn't at all the same fun person full of zeal and energy, and Becky called me out on it. "Pat, what happened? You've lost your spark; you need to get it back."

I listen and take heed to my friends when I know they care enough about me to speak the truth. I take heed and accept what they say with patience.

I got my spark back.

## *Talladega*

A few years back in 2006, when my boys were in school, and I was busy with life, I got a desperate call from a very dear friend of mine who was at a rather low point in her life.

My heart dropped as she told me her story. I just listened as my petrified heart and spirit went into deep prayer for my friend on the other end of the line.

Three hours of loving conversation later, I was well versed on some of her greatest dreams and desires. She adored NASCAR and driver, Tony Stewart. So off I went to purchase our tickets to the upcoming NASCAR race in Talladega, Alabama with prime seating in the pit area and a meeting with Tony Stewart. I had no idea what I signed up for, but we were on our way in my little convertible sports car to Talladega Super Speedway. I'll never forget the look on my boys' faces when I said, "Hey, I'm going to Talladega."

Shocked, they replied, "You're going where, Mom?"

Driving up in a sea of traffic in eight lanes all turning right into the same place, I edged my way over and found a passage, a shortcut to avoid waiting in between all the trucks to make my turn sooner than much later. In the middle of the lane stood a state trooper waving his hands at me, yelling for me to stop and turn around. I yelled back, "No! Why should I?" He yelled at me again, "You better turn around, lady!"

By then, my friend is practically under the seat wishing she were invisible as I'm screaming back at the top of my lungs, "Fuck you!" I flipped him off while turning my car back out into the crowd. I could not believe my behavior as I reluctantly turned back around to join back into the sea of redneck traffic.

Finally, we get inside just as the rain starts pouring down. We buy some orange ponchos, and she gets a picture of me with my headphones on backward with some guy behind me giving me a screwy look. I didn't know what I was in for or listening to for that matter.

We end up getting rained out, and I find us the very last available seedy motel room in the nearest town to Talladega for one hundred bucks.

What a dive, I thought as we rolled our suitcases by all the scary people. We quickly dead-bolted ourselves inside our room for the night.

The following day we headed back to watch the race only to wait longer in the huge parking lot to get out from all the traffic. I'll never forget parked and waiting behind this active van in front of us watching girls go in and out and the van going up and down with what I knew they surely were doing in there – so many girls lifting their tops showing their boobs for a string of beads. I did have beads, but I did not earn them.

I was proud of myself for being patient, for not bowing to peer pressure. I was proud of myself for waiting out that situation and that pride brought me peace.

This was a weekend of pure love and friendship, and an opportunity to practice patience minute by minute!

### *The Bahamas*

The first time in my life that I almost got arrested I was in Nassau with my teenage daughter and my husband's secretary. As a Regional Vice President, I had earned a week-long trip staying in a five-star resort with my daughter. I also secured a VIP room across from us for my consultant Lois. After a fun week-long trip, we were ready to return home getting to the airport two hours before takeoff.

While waiting for the flight, my daughter took our tickets up to the counter to make sure we had our seats together, but she returned without them. We got bumped, and there wasn't another flight back till the next day.

Lois still had her ticket and got on the plane while my daughter and I were standing there wondering what to do. All a sudden, she looks at me and says, "Let's just run and go get on the plane." I agreed and off we went running down the corridor.

My daughter said, "Mom, you are so cool, we're being just like Thelma and Louise!" as we ran out into the field and boarded the plane. We tap Lois on the shoulder, saying, "We're on. We made it."

Then much to our surprise came three rather large and oversized Bohemian policemen demanding we get off the plane. My daughter stood up and gave the most incredible heartwarming speech. "Please, would somebody give up their seats for my mom and me? I have finals in school I must get back to."

Nobody volunteered as we got escorted off the plane. I wanted to speak personally to the captain. As I stood out in the runway at the foot of the stairs to the plane, out comes, Lois crying and saying, "I just couldn't see leaving you girls here alone in this foreign country."

Finally, we made it to Miami. It was now past midnight, and we were in a long line of people. A family of five walked past everyone to the front of the line saying they were on the way to a funeral. My brave daughter speaks out, "Look; everybody's got issues and places they need to be. It's not fair to butt ahead."

There are no flights out for the next forty-eight hours, so we were stuck in Miami. The airline granted us transport to a hotel and provided breakfast, lunch, and dinner. We went out to get in the limo bus and guess who the other five passengers were waiting inside? Yes, they were the people on their way to a funeral.

### *I Love Being a Mom*

When my kids were in high school and going off to college, I liked to remain active in feeling close to them, so I joined social media. Joining was also good because the pictures and places replaced my physical photo albums later when I was traveling all over the world. I could post my whereabouts, so my family and friends could follow.

I found a memory post from precisely five years ago about how I'd taken up golf. Back then I felt that if I were to focus in on that little ball it would teach me patience and how to concentrate on one thing at a time. My post read:

*Hey... taking up golf... and I like it!*

*I'm reading Proof of Heaven by Eben Alexander (a brain surgeon who had a near-death experience). My favorite part so far is on page 41 "...and, It was not spoken in words, but he truly understood the message... You are loved and cherished, dearly, forever. You have nothing to fear. There is nothing you can do wrong...". I love this and feel this spoke to me as well— :) I'm going to apply this to every part of my life now, especially my golf game, LOL. So, I can't wait to play with you, Linda!*

This early morning, five years later, I'm making my coffee in my morning ritual, while I stand and wait in front of my fridge. I lean inward kissing the foreheads of my kids in pictures of us together and praying that God's hedge of protection surrounds us in his SPIRIT of light. Then by heart I recite over us what is written on a pad in pink tucked just underneath, "Do Something Awesome, you are loved, there is nothing you can do wrong, there is nothing to fear."

I patiently pray first thing every morning over all my children. It's my most favorite practice of love I give and receive for us, my precious family.

### *My Personal Patience Anecdote*

For the past five years, I have prayed over myself, kids, and my friends every morning.

Praying for our children, I feel is the greatest love you can give them. It's being true to myself in keeping my vows. Patience certainly is a virtue.

## *I Had Better Shape Up, 'Cuz I Need Myself*

Living in paradise, there's a certain rhythm and beat my fit and toned BODY desires being fed daily.

Along with being a dancer, life as a fitness coach and instructor enables my CHILD to act out and have the full freedom to display all her feisty moves. After all, this ADULT ego must get in her poolside hang-time in the sunshine to show off all her obvious results of hard work.

Must I always be thinking about how I must perform and be bringing my sexy back?

Much too often, I feel my energy level from within bursting rapidly at such a high speed that I can't explain or contain myself for that matter.

So, I went to an expert in the field of Energy, a psychic who came highly recommended by a group of professional ladies that I worked out with in my area of fitness. It was one of the most incredible, bizarre experiences I have ever felt. The psychic had her business located in her home in an upscale neighborhood. Her setup was inside the coolest round room I've ever seen. The cathedral ceiling was painted dark as night with the solar system: Mercury, Venus, Earth, Mars, Jupiter, Saturn, Uranus, the Big Dipper, Little Dipper, moon, and stars placed as if God made it himself.

In the very center was this comfortable, chic massage table where I laid flat on my back staring up into the magnificent outer space. Before we began, she discussed in detail how she would go about reading my energy. This was accomplished by spending twelve minutes on each of four sections, beginning with my head and then walking around my full body returning to make a full circle. She explained that she might lightly touch me with her hands. The moment she started; I felt the most incredible force of energy. It was unbelievable! The magnetic draw created a sensation between her hand

and my body, hovering no more than three inches in the distance above my head.

Finally, she spoke, "Wow, can you feel that?"

I responded, "Wow, yes, I can."

She then exclaimed, "I am not even touching you!" "I know," I replied.

It was so bizarre feeling electricity flying out from my body onto her fingertips, even without touching me and me just lying flat on my back patiently waiting for her diagnoses of what just transpired. She then said that I was the first in all her years of expertise to experience such a powerful force/source of energy felt between another human being without touch.

She was, indeed, blown away, and so was I.

Okay, so what does this mean? After all, I knew before going in that I'm high energy. What's a girl going to do with all that stuff, all that stuff, the energy, inside myself?

I know I came out of my mother's womb running! I was walking on my toes at six months. I see the picture before it's painted. I see the house before it's built. I see my book finished, so here I am only in the fourth chapter. I'm positive that my good friend Darla will chuckle in agreement with me and my issues when it comes to patience.

I am a work in progress, so when my ADULT ego barks out commands and demands on her teammates, a rush of compliance returns, "Yes, ma'am! No, ma'am! No excuse, ma'am! Aye, aye, ma'am! I'll find out, ma'am!"

CHILD trembles and panics with fear, reaching through for comfort only to find the stressed and hyper BODY. It's time to refuel.

Our energy is that inner force that drives us. Our body is the vehicle, and our core is our tank.

Step 1. Awareness – if I feel

Step 2. Action – I can heal

Step 3. Allow – and be real

*This is how I fight my battles.*

## 5. Kindness

*"If you propose to speak, always ask yourself, is it true, is it necessary, is it kind?" ~Buddha*

Kindness is a daily practice and gift that I begin with the first thing each day. As soon as my eyes open every morning, I rise with tender loving care to me first.

Being kind to myself within enables me to walk in the purest form of connection that I extend genuinely and lovingly throughout my day to others.

Yes, when I walk in the presence of love, joy, peace, and patience, kindness is then ingrained as a significant attribute that others see instantly in me. Especially with children, just one look is all it takes and its automatic love. Babies and children sense and know that they're safe with me. My gift and the most passionate job I do and have is working with children. Being present in the company of children enables my soul to be fresh, ready, and young. Together, our spirits play as one.

Meanness to myself occurs when I absorb the emotions of others, and I can feel them in my stomach. I call them my dark uglies. I stew in my endless head drama chattering along, endlessly recirculating through each pain in some effort to make it better. After all, I know the way and my head insists I can think myself into the solution. Shh, shh, now be quiet, Ms. Ego.

Hmmm, as I am writing this book for me, first, and then you, I am learning to set boundaries by listening to my gut. After all, they say the stomach is our second brain that can sense surrounding information, an energy that our eyes cannot see. When there's no self-respect or healthy boundaries how can I get respect from others?

*This is how I fight my battles.*

My Personal Kindness Mantra:

Step 1. Awareness – if I feel

Step 2. Action – I can heal

Step 3. Allow – and be real

I am the only one who can teach you how to treat me. These are my personal, real, true-life stories below, illustrating acts of kindness with patience and peace, joy, and love and how they all work together to make life better. I was born to be a dancer, and my favorite moves are with the children and people I love. I dance!

### *Kindness Pays Well*

I have learned that there are three types of people. Number one, there are trainable people. They want to learn everything there is to know about the business. I love working with trainable people. I mean, what's not to love?

Then there are the know-it-alls. They constantly interrupt you with what they think you need to hear, ruining the training for everyone else. I tend to avoid them like the plague.

The third, and last but not least, is the dud. They have no intention of doing the business and only signed up for a good deal on the products.

However, you can never underestimate the dud. After all, that was me.

That was part of my pre-framing in training when I would interview potential consultants to be on my team. So, if they were a know it all, they still had time to change. I chose my team wisely.

So how did I go from being a dud to a Regional Vice President earning a Mercedes as my ride along with hundreds of people working on my team and traveling on exotic trips for my family and me?

One stormy, rainy day, my neighbor's car broke down, and she asked me if I'd give her a ride to a hotel to see about a business opportunity. I said, "Sure." It was pouring down buckets of rain, so instead of waiting out in my car, I decided to go in. I wrote a check and bought the start-up kit; I sensed a good deal, even if I was a dud.

A month later, after selling a ton of skincare products, I was up on stage as a newly promoted District Manager receiving beautiful jewelry in a grand five-star hotel on Capitol Hill. I was clueless about what I was getting into in earning this four-day trip called an MTS (management training seminar). I was just happy to escape and get a break from my full-time job; I was constantly changing my boy's nasty diapers as a stay-at-home mom.

After the onstage fun, I headed upstairs. I was unlocking my hotel room door with anticipation of chillin' in my birthday suit all by myself in my own space. There inside sat this beautiful lady on one of the double beds smiling up at me, purring with a lovely, "Hello, you must be Patricia, my roommate."

You could about picture the shocked and disappointed look written all over my face. She sure did. I then managed to flatly say, "I thought I had my own room. There must be a mistake."

Twenty-five years later and we are still laughing about that. She was and is another one of my closest and precious friends, Dez.

Not only was I not prepared in knowing that I had a roommate, but I also hadn't packed suitably for the event activities. I didn't have an evening gown for dinner and my onstage recognition.

But guess what? My new friend was ready. In fact, she had brought two evening gowns, an extra one just in case. A former beauty queen, she had worked closely with the Miss America Pageants. She not only dressed me but did my hair and makeup too! Oh, what a trip. We bonded watching *Pretty Woman* that night filling the air with non-stop girl talk.

Later, I found out that ninety people replied to the advertisement placed in the Sunday paper. I was the first to become a manager in the city and state. None of those ninety people did anything in the business. I never saw the ad. I was being kind in giving my neighbor a lift in the storm. That act of kindness is still active today. It provided me with a career for my family (when my kids were just babies), an excellent income, trips all over the world and the ability to be a stay-at-home mom who worked my business from home.

### *Getting Fired from Teaching Sunday School*

In 2011, I was an empty nester and missing my kids; I decided that I would volunteer to teach the twelve-year-old's Sunday school sessions. The church would have their weekly chosen material all ready for me to teach. My husband loved this church mainly because the pastor was a retired all-star quarterback from a big university and his wife had been a cheerleader. Often, I would sit there, glancing over at her, watching her head nodding to sleep. I too was bored out of my mind.

But Sunday school was the place to be, especially for me. We would sing and listen to music and dance about the room, wrestling and playing, having a blast. When I first started teaching, I'd quickly go over their uninteresting and blah material. Then we'd get down to the serious goods to feed our souls. I was quite amazed that not one of my students knew the Lord's Prayer. My heart and soul told me that part of my mission for these kids, and the most critical job I had, was to teach them how to pray one of God's most meaningful prayers. "Our Father" ... Matthew 9:6-13.

Once, I even got permission and took all my kids to a nursing home nearby. It was a life-changing experience for all of us. When the following Sunday came, my happy-faced kids could hardly wait their turn to stand proudly before the class and recite their "Our Father" prayer. We celebrated, of course actively with joy, allowing our energy to connect our SPIRIT within. I then found myself purchasing twenty- two journals to reward my kids' hard work and study. In each of them, I wrote a personal message of their uniqueness written just under their name at the top.

After I got fired for making too much of a disturbance and because the Children's classroom was just upstairs over the sanctuary, a father of one of my students came running after me with a journal under his arm. He had tears running down his cheeks as he went on to tell me that his son would rarely speak and never shared in family conversations. When he opened the journal to show me his son's beautiful handwriting, I saw pages of his most heartfelt words, and I knew my mission was accomplished. My feelings were not hurt in being fired because it was merely a little stop for me taking care of business on my pathway to freedom. I knew I wasn't a fit in that church, but I fit in perfectly for that little boy in Sunday school.

## *Feelings Versus Numbness*

Before my wake-up call, you'll read later about that, I had been prescribed and tried just about every antidepressant on the market. I'll never forget the day I realized they worked.

I was a Regional Vice President managing Consultants, District and Area Managers throughout the USA. One of my team Consultants, Iris, had written me a business check (for a rather substantial amount) that had bounced. When she called to apologize, I simply responded with, "That's okay, sweetie, I understand. Don't you worry. Send me a new check when you've got funds in the bank."

After our sweet conversation ended, I hung up the phone and thought to myself, damn these pills work. I feel fantastic. Plus, I learned that kindness helped me be patient with her. I didn't explode or demand immediate payment. I could wait for the new check to come. Eventually, a new check came and cleared.

Now, that consultant is one of my dearest and closest friends. She is also by far one of the kindest people I know. We began our travels in business, and soon after they became business and family combined. I would target major cities all over the USA, where my mom, dad, cousins, and friends lived. She is part of my family.

When we surround ourselves with kind people, the contagious energy of happiness is shared and multiplied.

## *Sniper Attacks*

One of our business and family trips took place in October 2002. My friend, Iris, loved Maryland and Washington, D.C., especially in the fall. We planned to meet at Baltimore Washington International Airport, do a little shopping, and get a bite to eat, then head off to the beach in O.C. She pulled up and surprised me by renting a shiny red convertible. We were on our way to Ocean City, Maryland, with me behind the wheel and our hair blowing in the wind.

The beltway seemed empty; oddly, there was no traffic. I sensed a weird and eerie feeling in the air, especially when I pulled up to get gas noticing some people running and hiding but didn't think much more of it as I happily drove off. I then called my aunt to let her know I'd be running a little late since we had a two and a half to three-hour drive. She then warned me to do the speed limit, especially in the area close to the condo.

My cell phone rang with my aunt on the other end, wanting to know where we were. I let her know we'd be arriving within ten minutes. Still stopped on the side of the road from officer giving me a speeding ticket, I looked over and smiled at my friend. "Let's keep this one between us, okay?"

When we arrived close to midnight, my aunt had the news playing on the television. We had been under attack by anthrax in the air, and gunshots were fired by the Beltway Sniper, and all this happened in our traveling vicinity.

Pretty crazy, huh? We had no idea that we had been that close to the horrific and deadly crime scenes.

I believe we were safe because of the beauty of our friendship. We were visiting family and friends with lovingkindness surrounding us.

### *The Bad News*

Under normal circumstances, I purposely avoid watching the news. I refuse to allow all that negative information to take root in my head. I don't have cable, but I do turn on my Roku to occasionally watch a documentary on Netflix.

On occasion, I am forced to watch. For example, when I'm volunteering at the Children's Hospital, it is not uncommon to have blaring in the background the news or some live stream of people airing out all their dirty laundry. I may periodically give a glance up, but only for a second or two to remind me of why I am careful about what I allow into myself.

After watching my mom's habits and witnessing firsthand how she slowly began to deteriorate, I try to take a different route. The first thing she'd do in the morning was read the paper. Then she'd have that TV blaring out back and forth from the Weather Channel to the local news and then switch to world news. She was so consumed and caught up in all of that she had barely enough energy and room to want to hear about me and my life. I don't know if there is a way to avoid the deadly disease of Dementia and Alzheimer's. However, for me, overloading and allowing devastating news that has absolutely nothing to do with me seems a grave detriment to my SPIRIT. I can't stop the weather, I can't stop the evil, nor could my mother.

In one of my last visits with her when she was still in her house, she hadn't gone out of her home for over a year. She stayed inside with the drapes drawn, and the television volume turned up. I couldn't stay there. I stayed in a hotel nearby. In her bedroom she had a sweater hung over the screen of her television. She told me that it was there to block and stop the man that keeps trying to get her by coming in through the screen. Before dementia, my mother had the kindest heart. She would give a stranger the shirt off her back, and there was always room at our table for others at dinner time. To see her paranoid and suspicious of others, where she had once been so open and giving, made me incredibly sad. It showed me that disease could sometimes take kindness away.

## *Will I Ever Stop Missing Him?*

In March 2019, I'd been alone in paradise for six months. I'm still feeling a bit lonely in missing my Aussie boyfriend. I had started a habit of watching a DVD nightly and falling asleep with it on. So, when I must be at work by 6:00 a.m., I tend to wake up every two to three hours throughout the night.

After having my daily chat with my close friend, Darla, sharing my latest material about my book along with my strange sleeping patterns, she immediately advised me to get rid of the blue light effects by unplugging all the electronics in my bedroom. She did the same a while back and said it is amazing how she's read three books in the recent weeks and sleeping easily through the night.

It's something I already knew but had forgotten. Hmmm.

Kindness and simple sharing save the day again. Because I genuinely practiced kindness with my team, *My Fight Club Within*, came to fruition.

*This is how I fight my battles.*

## 6. Goodness

*"Have courage and be kind. For where there is kindness there is goodness, and where there is goodness there is magic." ~Cinderella*

Patience and kindness and goodness, oh my! It's so plentiful for me and you; why? Because it's free, and it's everywhere. It's good to be alive. I so look forward to waking up each day, being grateful that I can rise while watching out my window as the sun peeks up over the water. I may then spend some time meditating, maybe take a walk on the beach or a bike ride and purposefully go out of my way to smile while giving eye contact and greeting others, saying good morning to as many peeps as I can. I love spending time with being kind to myself and having plenty of goodness that is genuinely and gracefully coming out of me and ricocheting amongst others.

However, I also realize that I must understand that I'm not going to feel good all the time. After all, I remember, I'm only human.

Selfishness is giving love to get love. However, oh, how I quickly discovered it only leaves me empty and never satisfied. Meeting everybody else's needs sometimes meant I didn't meet my own. I was needy for conditional love. This causes constant havoc on my BODY while at the same time imprisoning me inside my head. Currently, my head is no friendly place to be, now the isolated boxing ring with mindless CHILDhood tantrums warring with my fearful ADULT ego, refusing to allow my true SPIRIT to free me. BODY is currently dazed and confused, screaming out with pain, "Please, stop your fighting!"

Here I go, headlong into the next round of suffering. Damn, it hurts, and it hurts badly. I choose to face it and not run away. I remember that everybody suffers, and millions are suffering at this very moment. I'm not alone, and I am only human. I am going to switch on my light, group hug, cry if I must, and maybe get on my knees on the side of my bed and beat my pillows for five minutes. I will feel this sorrow and heartbreak to the fullest extent. However, I will not be stuck, and this will be a short round. Sometimes I find the hardest battle is between what I know in my head and feel in my heart.

*This is how I fight my battles.*

### **We Are All One-of-a-Kind**

I find it fascinating how we are all so uniquely built, so readily equipped within, with all our own magnificent and outstanding talents. We all have our very own personal, deeply rooted, well ingrained one- of-a-kind desires and passions that may only be accepted from within one's self. No one can fulfill and live your one-of-a-kind life and soul desires but that awesome you. A discovery I made during my journey from within and without is that although we are all uniquely built individuals, we are all still very much the same. Meaning we are all living and breathing in and out one breath at a time, with a heart beating one beat at a time, dancing in time every day to the same twenty-four hours, but to the beat of whom?

As I carry on here with my words on these pages, I desire to address and expound upon many of the unspoken thoughts and concepts that we deem as shameful and embarrassing. My life experiences I humbly share, and bare here, for this purpose, in this very book. You'll see it all; the good, the bad and the ugly; for example, the three P's – Poop, Puke, and Pee. Let's agree to agree that it's a given that it does and will happen to us, at least one of them, every single day. Ever in your wildest dreams or thoughts have you wanted to do that for somebody else? For your partner, child, or friend? Alternatively, reverse it here; would you ever think about asking someone to do yours?

It's good that we all poop, puke, and pee. We are all human beings, and these are the experiences that make us unique, and we all have this in common.

Let's talk about my three E's – Emotions, Energies, and Egghead. Let's agree to agree that it's a given that these things are each displayed by you and me every moment of every day.

Why not now go inside the ring (your ring, not mine), with your ADULT ego (egghead), CHILD (emotions), BODY (energies), and SPIRIT (your freedom).

So far, you have a pretty good idea of my issues. What are yours?

- How many turds are you still eating?
- How pissed off are you at yourself and others for taking all their crap out on you or your crap for that matter?
- How much more will you take of others' puke and venom on you?

Let's now add the three S's – Sex, Saint, and Suffering.

We are all sexual beings. For me, though, it goes hand-in-hand with love. I cannot separate love, sex, and my emotions.

My love juice is very sacred and personal.

The first time I discovered this was the most awkward encounter with a creepy old man sitting on a park bench. My girlfriend and I were around twelve years of age and were walking through the park after school one sunny day.

Sitting on a park bench, we both gazed over at this older man staring back at us with his little dog on a leash. He then said, "I'll give you girls a quarter if you want to watch the white stuff come out."

As he said that, he started pulling out his penis, and we both took off running. Out of breath and creeped out, I realized it was time to use my very own kept emergency quarter. Yes, it was a top priority for me to carry this quarter and always have it tucked safely in my key case. I called my dad who advised us to run to the police station, and he would be there "pronto." Half a dozen cops along with my dad went combing the park to find the man and his dog. They never found him.

I often thought about that sad, perverted man and how he exposed himself by jerking off in front of little girls, creeping them out with his little penis and drips of semen.

It made me think about myself, and if I were to have a juice-like substance come out of my body that I would keep it personal. It would be kept sacred to be a treasure, only to be shared and seen between my husband-to-be and me.

### *F Word*

I'll never forget the day when I was maybe six years of age, and I was visiting my mom on a Sunday. I was playing at the local neighborhood schoolyard, swinging on the swings, and hanging on the monkey bars. This older boy came over to me and said, "I want to take you over to the sandbox and fuck you."

I said, "No," and quickly ran away back to my mom's house.

I kept that to myself, until later, when my dad and his friend were walking with me to buy a snow cone. I asked, "Daddy, what does the word fuck mean?"

Startled, he replied, "What did you just ask me?"

I repeated, "What does the word fuck mean?"

He then asked me as to why am I asking him about this word? I told him the story about how this boy wanted to fuck me in the sandbox at the neighborhood schoolyard by my mom's house. That was the day I got my first lesson and learned that that was a bad word and a bad thing and never to allow anybody to do that to me.

### Acts of Evil

It was in the summer; I was fifteen years old and hanging at my mom's house for a couple of weeks. My mom helped me get a job as a shampoo girl working in the local beauty salon.

The owner of the salon was a very handsome middle-aged man that was married to a very beautiful woman.

You might imagine my shock and surprise after finishing up work one day as I was awarded another peek into the depths of errant ways.

I was alone with the owner when all of a sudden, he looks over at me and says, "Patty, do you know how sometimes you may see a basket of apples, and some may have brown spots from bruising, some may have holes with worms, and some are just too rotten and ripe? But then you take notice and see the shiniest and most beautiful one is sitting right there in front of you to pick and enjoy for your pleasure?"

"No," I said.

He said, "Well, that's how I feel about you. I want you so badly, more than anything else in this world."

At that very moment, I flew out of there as fast as I could.

## *Horrified*

I moved in with my mom at the age of sixteen. My mom was taking a two-week vacation, leaving me alone but instructed me to stay at my friend's house.

My friend was very promiscuous, free, and open when pertaining to sex. I never judged her, and I loved her dearly and still do. We were opposites, though as I was a little saint and goody two-shoes, one of the last virgins in high school. I would share my dates with her. I know that probably sounds like the weirdest and most outlandish thing, but it wasn't at all that way for me.

For example, a boy that liked me would take me on a date to a movie, and I would be kind and invite my friend to join us. The date would be winding down with the three of us walking me home. Sometimes we'd stop on the way at one of our houses where the parents were gone. I can remember waiting outside in the living room for my friend and my date to finish up.

She would then later apologize to me telling me how sorry she was, but I felt sorry for her, and it didn't matter to me because after all, sex, making love, for me would be sacred. Besides, that boy didn't matter to me, and he wasn't at all meant to be for me.

In the two weeks I stayed with her and her family, it became apparent precisely why my friend behaved as she did. It was a Saturday afternoon, and her mom was at work. Her dad just had back surgery and was recovering at home with the two of us. We were hungry and wanted to get pizza. My friend had just gotten her driver's license and would get so excited when she'd get to take the car out for a spin. Her dad gave her the keys and allowed her to take the car, but she was to go alone, and I was to stay there. She then grabbed the keys and left me there alone with her dad.

I felt eerie and dark feelings beginning to rise, just like I had felt before in the beauty salon. I just sprung up off the couch, and I said I needed to go. He then ran over and got ahead of me, blocking the front door with his body, and said, "You're not going anywhere."

I got in his face, kicked him, and shoved his sorry little ass out of my way. I pushed through the doorway and didn't stop running until I got to my mom's house. I was devastated, not really with what just happened to me, because nothing did, but with the evil and hell in which my good friend had to live.

My friend had gone home with the pizza only to find me missing. She figured out that I would probably be three blocks away at my mom's. We then went to her mom and told her what had happened. She looked me straight in the eyes and called me a liar claiming she didn't believe me because "He's got a bad back."

My friend cried out, "No, Mom, Patty is telling the truth!" Tears bursting out of her, she continued, "Mom, it is true. She's telling the truth. How do I know? Because Dad has raped me over and over and over again."

My heart was utterly broken that day for my friend. It made perfect sense as to why she was like she was. I finally got it and understood totally.

There would be no apology accepted or allowed by my friend on behalf of her dad to me. Never would I expect my friend to be sorry or apologize to me for the evil acts of her dad. Nor did I want her to experience any guilt for leaving me alone with that monster. I only wanted her to be encouraged that it was supposed to happen so she could stop it and begin to turn her life around.

Not too many years after that, when my kids were babies, I was visiting my mom and dad. My friend and I got together, and she told me the horrible news about how her father had been killed. He was decapitated in a head-on collision. Her mom, who had stuck by her husband's side, had gone blind. My exact reply to my friend was, "I can't believe what I'm feeling and about to say and speak out loud to you, but I must confess, I'm not at all sorry for your dad's death. He got what he deserved for how he treated you. Your mom, too, for not defending and protecting her daughter from her husband's monstrous acts. I'm sorry, girl, but I feel absolutely no sympathy for your mom and dad." All I could feel was my friend's terror, horrific pain, and the suffering she had endured at the hands of her parents. She understood. I think that if ever there was an earth angel, she was mine.

### *My Parents*

I needed my parents to survive. I would have died as a child without their connection in being my mom and dad. I stayed connected at all costs with whatever they gave me. I called it love. If daddy called me a bad girl, daddy was right. I will cook and clean and make daddy happy; then he'll love me. So, when I am feeling sad and alone, I do more things to make daddy love me. I go into these feelings from when I was a child. My style for coping would be to run away. I would run to mommy.

*My Fight Club Within* is teaching and training me to experience and feel. This crap landed on me from childhood. I had to be a survivor, and I survived. Love from within is being good to myself in total truth about how I'm feeling. Suffering is part of my healing. I must feel to heal. My power shift is when I talk about how my fight club inside experiences group hugs, crying, but most importantly, awareness of the three A's that you'll find mentioned in almost every chapter. The power shift occurs when I feel my feelings, and they change. Just like the clouds shift, the sensations will move to aliveness when I feel them and acknowledge them. Then, I'm no longer stuck in a rut, for they will move.

## *Dad*

My dad wasn't the easiest man to live with by any means. Later on, I will write about some of my dad's monstrous acts toward me. However, I have forgiven my dad for his crazy insanity and feel totally blessed to have been raised by him. He sheltered me with discipline and was quite strict regarding how to take care of myself. He took great care to teach me how to honor myself by being truthful with my actions and words. He spoke at length regarding respect for me and others. To give my time in helping the less fortunate was expected. He taught me how to dance as I was his partner in his practice at dance school. It was very important to him how our home was to be kept and honored as our sanctuary, our safe place. Never once did he ever bring women to stay all night or alcohol into our home. Not once have I ever seen my dad drunk. Grace was spoken daily as we blessed and were grateful for every meal we prepared and ate together.

The value of commitment was learned through example. He never left me cold or out in the dark. I always had a key, comfort from the ever-burning front porch light, and welcoming arms to embrace me. He told me every day of our life together that I was loved. My parents divorced when I was five, so they lived in separate houses.

## *Mom*

With Mom, I had the extreme opposite. It wasn't until she was in her seventies when she would begin telling me she loved me. I trained her by saying, "I love you, Mom," after every phone conversation. Finally, one fine day, she reciprocated. I didn't have a key to her place. Her front door would be locked, and the porch light turned off if I wasn't home by a certain time. I would have to sleep on the front porch.

There were many uneventful times when my mom would be heavily intoxicated, driving under the influence with me riding beside her, the terrified and powerless passenger. Fairly regularly, we spent time together in the bathroom, me holding her hair back to avoid her vomit, feeding her ice chips and saltine crackers to nurse her hangovers. She lived with an alcoholic boyfriend, and she would sometimes drink just as much as him.

Spending hours in my bedroom, I would put on my headphones to avoid hearing her arguing with her alcoholic boyfriend who often would beat her up. I would have to keep an ear open to listen for her shout out to me to call the police to come. She would kick him out only to have him back inside by my next Sunday visit. That Sunday would usually be tamer than we would maybe take a pleasant family drive in the country, and there would be no alcohol; thank God!

The worst part was her constant lying and then in return, trying to get me caught up in her web of deception. Her most famous line was, "Let's get the story straight between us so we'll be on the same page."

I would keep silent and never join in. Less was best. I hated dishonesty and would never agree to partake in her wicked schemes. She did have a heart of gold when it came to caring for me when I was sick. She always made me feel better. She was also the best cook ever. As much as she hated my dad, she always snuck me out with a hot plate of food to take home to him, so he too got to enjoy the best of my mom's Sunday cooking.

### *Mom and Dad Together for Me*

I'll never forget my experience with getting my tonsils out. Here I was, an eight-year-old little girl in the hospital bed unable to speak, sore throat, with my mom and dad on each side of me. My dad was reading me a storybook about a parrot; I've always been fascinated with birds, as my mom was being disruptive by whispering in my ear, "Make sure you keep this a secret and don't tell your dad."

My mother was always gossiping and running down my dad and whispering in my ear and was always trying to get me to lie. I hated it.

Little did she know at a very young age, I learned how to tune her out. I taught myself how not to take in her lame, fucked up information. And, yes, I knew at the tender age of eight how to use that swear word in a sentence. However, never out loud!

### *My Parents Were Fun-Loving*

In my last chapter on kindness, I wrote about my sweet friend Iris, who underwent the sniper-anthrax attacks with me. She is one of my few friends who would travel and stay with me at my mom's place and then my dad's. She loved and adored my parents, and they loved and adored her. We shared so many good and happy times with my mom and dad, but separate, three by three. However, double the fun of togetherness, just like my childhood holidays, I'd always get two.

My sweet, kind-hearted friend Iris taught me over time to notice and appreciate the many good qualities that my parents had in them. My friend would go to Mass and then dance the night away at the Moose Club with my dad and me. Then we'd go hang out with my mom canning tomatoes, with Mom making us her special Greek salads and having crab feasts in her backyard. My mom created in her handwriting three containers of all her yummy and delicious Sunday best recipes for me, my daughter, and my best friend, Iris. That was her way of saying, "I love you," to us. Goodness Rules!

Step 1. Awareness – if I feel

Step 2. Action – I can heal

Step 3. Allow – and be real

*This is how I fight my battles.*

## 7. Faithfulness

*"Faithful is Being Steadfast in Affection or Allegiance; Loyal" ~ from Merriam Webster Dictionary*

Faithfulness is being true to myself as I remind myself daily of that beautiful commitment and vow, I made to myself. Faithfulness always goes hand-in-hand with accountability. I hold myself accountable by investing in myself.

In March 2018, I attended the most incredible life-changing program called the *Hoffman Process*. The *Hoffman Process* is a week-long healing retreat of transformation and development for people who feel stuck in one or more important areas of their life. These were the best ten days of my entire life and by far, one of the most significant investments that I have ever gifted to myself. Selling my diamond earrings and exchanging that energy for this process delivered life-changing results for me.

Even operating to the best of my ability, I have learned to ask for help. I get therapy and seek out assistance when I feel stuck inside a boxing round too long. It's a beautiful gift to be faithful, accountable and true-to-self by receiving help when I need it. Outstanding results can then occur, getting me back on track, resulting in again walking in faith with love to myself and others. I committed to myself in the first chapter of this book, and I'm holding true and keeping my vows.

The true manifestation of my SPIRIT allows for walking and dancing with so much love, joy, peace, patience, kindness, and goodness while cherishing every moment. Disregarding these truths can stop me in my tracks with a sudden, dark, and ugly string of lies that pops into my head. "I'm just not enough. I don't deserve this. I made a foolish mistake in marrying me."

"Oh, Patricia Ann, remember that faithful vow I made to you?" I lovingly remind myself.

When I was pregnant, I enjoyed writing poetry and singing to my babies. So, from a very young age, we would sing and create songs, joining in our unique flavor of words together in a loving expression of harmony. I have just recently begun to sing again a new song.

### *God. Where Are You?*

In my last chapter entitled, "Goodness," I shared the tragic story about my best friend in high school and how she displayed her great strength and courage by standing up and speaking the truth for me, her friend, although she had never stood up for herself.

No one would give her the time of day. I was her only friend, after all, she had a bad reputation. We were connected by her goodness; I knew her deeply, beyond her so-called bad reputation, despite not knowing at the time what her dad was doing to her.

That was when I first started questioning my faith in God. Why did he allow my good friend to suffer such horror and by her very own father? I felt I didn't receive answers, and more or less told God to piss off.

My best friend and I would communicate and talk about everything, and I mean everything. So even though I was still a virgin, I wanted to know how to make love and be prepared for when that special day would come. So, I would pick my friend's brain, and she would teach me giving me lessons, verbally of course, on how to be a lover. After all, I felt after many hours of waiting on her and observing all these happy-faced boys, that my friend was indeed the best.

We went on to share many, many more awesome times. We had our very own language, nicknames we created in a foreign slang for each other and our special songs where we meshed our bizarre words with popular melodies. We even had our very own famous dance, and whenever we would see each other from a distance, we'd bring it – our own flavor of groovy moves. We were always our outrageously silly and goofy selves together. We were dorks and proud of it.

### *Being Silly*

One of the funniest and silliest things we did was trying to find out where this cute boy lived that we liked. So, I came up with the bright idea to write down our telephone number on a piece of paper, wrap the paper around a rock, and bind it tightly with a rubber band. We threw it up on the porch of the house we thought was his and awaited our call. Well, as you may imagine, it didn't go down as planned. I had thrown the rock so hard that it went straight ahead past the porch and through the window of the wrong house. The boy lived next door.

So, we got a call all right; a call from a stranger demanding that I pay for the broken window. My mom was furious and made me pay out of my pocket. I was faithful to my mother's wishes.

Luckily for me, it just so happened to be that I was the neighborhood salesperson for my mom's neighborhood. That was the beginning for me in developing my ability as a salesman. Well, not the entire hood, only my mom's next-door neighbor to the right and the family across the street. They were all my best customers. I loved these people; they were my pretend parents and siblings.

Next door, the couple had five children, and directly across the street they had six. They were all older than me, so I was kind of like their youngest sibling, the baby. All the kids had their mom and dad together as a real family. I felt special being spoiled, but I was still missing my dad. When I was there, their dad became my dad and would even buy most of the items I had for sale. I had attractive products mainly because my dad always had nice tools and gadgets. He was an inventor and would make me cool stuff. He bought many unique watches for me, so I always knew the time. I always had quite nice, one-of-a-kind merchandise to sell.

One of my dad's inventions was a burglar alarm system for our house. We had three attempted break-ins. During the third attempt, my dad had come home to find the stranger and chased after him. Running through the field behind our home, the thief dropped all our goods to the ground as he escaped.

Our security system alarm was a ship horn located in our basement. It was wired to an electric box installed upstairs on our closed-in porch and activated, illuminating a small light, with the turn of a tractor key. There were no further attempted break-ins at our home after that. However, my dad would have fun with letting the whole neighborhood know when I was coming home late and even getting a kick out of using it to get my attention, but I see that he was faithful to me, to his responsibilities to keep me safe.

## *My Two Worlds*

I felt special because I had the best of both worlds. It was as if I was a member and part of two different tribes filled with love and support. In my one world at my mom's and then in my other world at my dad's.

My neighbors next door to my dad's house were Catholic like us and just so happened to be another full house. They were a family of love, having awesome parents with six kids and me fitting beautifully six months in between my two best playmates – my sisters. They leaned heavily on their faith in God.

## *My Safe Home*

The house I grew up in was the house my grandfather bought as a wedding present for my mom and dad. I was five when my mom left my dad and me.

My dad lived out his beliefs and faithfulness to the church; he never remarried and died alone in our house. In 2005, the next-door neighbor, Ms. Sue, had called me with the sad news. My dad had given me all the directions for his funeral months before. In fact, we even rehearsed it, making sure I wouldn't get lost in finding the funeral home. I hardly had to do anything except mail the invitations.

He was an only child, and his mom and dad were well off. My grandmother was Jewish, and my grandfather was German. They were a very tight-knit family, dedicated to the church. They owned a rather large neighborhood community of fifty plus single-family homes and a relatively successful dry-cleaning business. My dad was born in a large and beautiful, upper-class home. His actual birth took place inside that home, as did the entirety of his childhood. He lived his whole life in only two houses within a five-mile radius of each other. My grandparents were also the proud owner of a beautiful shore home with a yacht docked at their pier. My grandfather built and founded the Catholic Church where my dad attended parochial school. I attended that school as well.

When I look back at my dad's life, I can fully understand that he lived it to the best of his ability. Although his faith was strong and committed to the Catholic religion, he missed out on what all this religion was initially based.

We regularly partook in substantial discussions on this touchy topic. Especially after I found myself exploring many different churches, did this very type of discourse arise between us. I found myself delving ever more in-depth on the subject, studying the original Greek and Hebrew manuscripts. I was like a bee plunged deeply into the flower seeking the sweet nectar of truth and firm answers.

I never showed any disrespect to my father by dishonoring him and his beliefs. In fact, I would attend mass at his church when visiting, and he would do the same for me.

His was great faith indeed, but over time I watched bitterness, shame, and guilt rob him of his peace of freedom. He lived abiding all too deeply in pain and anger towards my mom, along with the rules of his church. My dad's faithfulness demonstrated dearly his commitment to the Catholic Church, his steadfast belief in God, and his continuing care of me. However, I was a constant reminder of my mother and how she left him.

My beliefs slowly solidified after studying and spending much time on this subject matter. History has recorded that religion was around long before Jesus ever walked the earth. After all, it was the religious group of the Pharisees that crucified him.

Regarding having a relationship with God, Buddha, or any form of a personal Higher Power, that meaning your choice in the spiritual realm of belief, I feel that it should be experienced with the embrace of unconditional love – a connection equaling nothing less than total uplifting of enlightenment.

Sometimes in my life, I would find myself angry at God, but the feeling didn't last very long.

I got the understanding and answer that I needed to my question, "How can God allow bad things to happen?"

My answer:

God is Spirit. Spirit/God is Omni.

God is Love. There is no hate in God.

God is Perfect. There is no sin in God.

God is light. There is no darkness in God.

God is timeless. God is the Alpha and Omega.

This is my perspective and what I believe to be true for me as far as my faith and personal relationship to the Creator. My belief is quite simple. I know I am loved; I know there's nothing I can do wrong, and there's nothing for me to fear. For me, there is no limitation on communication with God. Sometimes, and maybe you can relate, I find myself simply crying out, "Oh God!" I feel he is everywhere all the time. Being a God of Light, it is impossible for darkness to touch or enter him for he is the Light, Highest High of all.

I believe that beyond all our human senses of touch, hearing, and smell, that our soul/spirit are timeless in being just like God. God, being a spirit, can only connect with us in the present, where light can only exist. Although our bodies will die, our spirit lives on throughout all eternity.

Our universe/atmosphere engulfs us (our Spirit) as one as in the air we breathe, our ambiance, aroma, aura, climate, flavor, karma, odor, nimbus, patina, smell, temper, vibrations. How can Spirit (God) of Light cause (evil) darkness in this world to me? It is scientifically/spiritually impossible. I can't blame the air, the sun, the moon, or the stars either.

This is simply how I feel about my part in connection with the universe, my atmosphere in sharing my deepest love from within.

I am a firm believer that having a parent, grandparent, great grandparent, etc., who pray for their children, themselves, and others are the most powerful and spiritual act of love towards self and all mankind.

## *My Heaven*

Heaven, for me, is always within my reach, present here on earth. When we die, some people believe that we either go to another place such as Heaven or Hell, or we reincarnate.

I feel I will be reconnected and meeting all my family of loved ones such as my great grandmother who silently and lovingly prayed over me for the first six months of my life. I was destined to die in my first month of existence in ICU, quarantined, and strapped down in my incubator covered in boils from high fever, next to eleven other babies.

I was told by my mother how excruciating it was to see me through a window with my tiny little feet and hands tied down while watching the doctor with scalpel in hand lancing open the boils. Four of the babies died, and I was a lucky one that made it through.

My great grandmother's faithfulness lives on and is my greatest treasure as I do the same for my children and all my beloved; I pray.

I don't feel I have to go to a church building while reciting the same words over and over to him in a pew at a ritual mass service. To me, that is not a loving relationship. I could never imagine spending an hour a day with my significant other saying the exact same words over and over and over again. How boring?

I am not anti-church either, for I feel that fellowship and community are very important. In fact, I recently went out of my way to visit the Hillsong Church in Sydney, Australia and will admit I was a bit disappointed. I love their praise music and was blown away at the London Hillsong performance while visiting a couple years back. So, I found myself disappointed in Sydney on this trip since I was comparing, another one of my weaknesses.

My faithfulness is strong when I trust and allow my SPIRIT to lead my path...

Miracles have been happening, and still are, for me almost every moment of the day since October 2018 when I moved to Paradise. All too often, I must admit, I take them for granted.

I still have regular tears of frustration from pleading and crying out to God, "Why here God?" My loneliness whispers endless prayers even in my sleep.

I keep the faith in sharing with you that I am walking this journey out, especially as I write this chapter. It's just as important for me to write this as it may be to have written out for you.

I tend to get so caught up in being busy with busyness and getting the job done. Even in writing this book, I just wanted to hurry up and get it done. I thought I'd have it finished within a month, focusing on the future instead of being transparent and here right now with you. Looking for the result only detracts from experiencing and enjoying all the many blessings of our journey on these pages.

I guess you could say I am running again; running away with disappointment, thinking, "I'm no writer. Who will want to read this crapshoot? Who am I fooling?"

I just go about teaching my classes, working at the Castle, and volunteering once a week at the Children's Hospital. Then in all my spare time, I write. I'm tired. I am all work and no play.

In January 2019, I spent all day writing. I am in dire need of food, sunshine, and fun. So, I'm going inside my fighting ring to grab ahold of my crabby little CHILD, my fried egghead ADULT intellect, my sorry-ass, tired BODY and relinquish all this exhaustion and give it up to my SPIRIT.

I am going to be grateful for my awesome job working at the Castle with all the beautiful people from all walks of life; housekeepers, dishwashers, cooks, laundry handlers, bartenders, wait staff, managers, supervisors, coworkers, guests, and members. I love folding towels for the guests, making fruit water, and keeping the beautiful bowl filled with apples, oranges, and bananas. I especially enjoy making my class fiercely sweat during an incredible workout.

I am enormously honored to volunteer and work at the Children's Hospital with all the doctors, nurses, and families of all the precious children. My time is never better spent than when silently praying for their miracles of healing.

Let me state my gratitude as well for my spectacularly cozy waterfront apartment furnished with everything I need. There is food in my refrigerator, my car and bike in the carport and an iPhone, iPad, and MacBook Air to write my book for you and me. I have a healthy body to walk me to work and lungs to breathe the precious air.

I will appreciate, receive, and enjoy all these miracles that I have now encountered in just four short months of moving here to paradise, jobless, and not knowing a soul.

Now I will slip into a bathing suit, put on my flip-flops, cover up with sunscreen and enjoy this beautiful day as I continue my path of faithfulness to myself with SPIRIT leading my steps to total freedom.

## *My Four F Words – Faith, Fear, Fucked and Fix*

Have you ever been deeply fucked over? I know I certainly have. At the same time, I know I have deeply broken a heart or two.

I'm not narrowing it down here to just romantic relationships; I'm referring to all sorts of different people in general – partners, spouses, relatives, friends, strangers and even myself.

The aftermath is yet a contender, long after your struggles end. You may be on the giving or receiving end, or if it's you fucking yourself over, you may be getting it from both ends. You spend the rest of your days living in fear, shame, guilt and self-hatred, trying to fix yours, and possibly others fucked up lives. It's a vicious and endless cycle.

The definition of faith is trust in someone or something. Everyone must have faith daily whether they want to believe it or not. Just take an Uber ride for example, or even driving your car. When it inevitably breaks down, you must get it fixed.

You're fucked when you're stuck, and broken-down waiting, yet somehow you muster faith that someone will show up with a tow truck.

I know I have issues, and I am a work in progress. I also realize I have been getting carried away with using the F-bomb far too much. I vow to be faithful, loyal, and trusting to myself first. I have created healthy and safe boundaries.

### **Og Mandino**

When my babies were young in the 1990s, not long after my trip to Southern California, I returned home taking heed of what my best friend Becky had noticed missing in me, my spark.

I was attending a Management Training Seminar, and Og Mandino was our motivational speaker. I was obsessed with him and the beautiful message he spoke on from his book, *The Greatest Salesman in the World*. During the break, I waited in line at his book signing table. When it was my turn to meet him, I broke down with tears streaming down my face. He kindly took me behind the curtain so we could talk. I knew he was a dedicated Catholic man, so I opened up about my situation. I wanted my spark back, and I was tired of wearing my happy face mask.

Og said that while God hates divorce, it's the acts of behavior and ill-treatment that causes divorce and he doesn't expect anybody to suffer by staying in a marriage just for the sake of a religious rule. Marriage should be a unity of love and commitment and faithfulness.

It was the greatest counseling session. He shared so much love and compassion with no judgment. He spent forty-five minutes giving me so much wisdom and advice, much of which I have been sharing with you.

Step 1. Awareness – if I feel

Step 2. Action – I can heal

Step 3. Allow – and be real

*This is how I fight my battles.*

## 8. Gentleness

*"However many holy words you read, however many you speak, what good will they do you if you do not act on upon them?"* ~Buddha

Gentleness with me is key. Being an empath gives me a significant advantage in connecting with others because I have that built-in soul connection. I know and realize the importance of gentleness with myself firsthand as my energy is continually wanting to explode within. My gentle, loving spirit must be in control, leading me, because when I'm experiencing other people, their own issues quite easily take over, smearing me all over with the infamous harsh, dark uglies. They overwhelm my space and quickly send me in the fetal position. So, I have been stuck in that position sometimes for days.

When my mom was suffering from Alzheimer's, she forgot everybody; her husband, son, sisters, grandchildren, and friends – everybody but me. It was so bizarre because she knew me precisely as I was, and we would talk every single day on the phone. The hardest thing for me was that I felt her pain. However, being with her when she died was the most beautiful experience of our life together as mother and daughter. I allowed my SPIRIT to lead me, and it was there so very present with us. I will write more on this a little later in this book.

In 2018, my youngest son, John, and I were in deep conversation about my recent decision to live by the beach. John is my rock that I can always count on to be there for me.

He's a very successful family man, business owner and by far one of the smartest dudes I know. He took off from work, leaving his family with his older brother, Patrick, my middle son who flew in from California, to move me, driving the rental truck to the beach. They worked so hard transporting me to my new life.

John said to me, "Mom, why in the world are you moving so far away? You could live down the street in such a beautiful area and be close to me."

To which I replied, "I have spent the beginning of my life living with my dad, then my husband where he chose, and now I have been in Texas for you. I want to make a choice now to live where I want to live. I want to be near the water and nature. Please understand I am not selfish in leaving. You and your sister, Tatum, have your beautiful families here living your lives.

It's time for me to be on my own."

After the big move and before taking an early morning flight out, he hugged me ever so tightly and asked, "Mom, are you going to be okay here? You can always come back home."

I love that my son showed so much gentleness with me, so much love and caring. I also think that we must learn to be gentle with ourselves, and that's what I had to do by learning to live on my own.

*This is how I fight my battles.*

### *Family*

I spent twenty-three years committed and faithful to one man, my husband.

However, was I faithful to myself?

Not only was I a good wife, but I also loved and adored being a mother to my three amazing, beautiful children. There is absolutely no title or place higher in this world that means more to me than being "Mom" to my three kids. We were a five-unit family under the same roof. That was truly heaven to me.

Life was a whirlwind of busy-ness being a wife and a mother and having two boys was a challenge. Having an athletic husband as their coach was a big plus and I would focus more on the music and dance.

I bought an old upright piano for a hundred bucks when our boys were three and four. So, by the time they were seven and eight, they were performing duets before an audience of over fifty people at Baylor University, scoring excellent and superior on their performances. Some of my most beautiful memories were watching and listening to them practice piano in their dirty baseball and football uniforms for a half-hour each before me driving them to their lessons.

During lessons, I would wait for them. I'll never forget how one of their favorite piano teachers talked me into learning how to play "Amazing Grace." She would have me practice in another room while teaching my boys. I wanted to learn that song, so I could play it at my Uncle Paul's funeral. He was a talented artist and died suddenly from pancreatic cancer. Everybody loved him as he was one of the kindest and gentlest man you'd ever want to meet.

The church was packed as I was called up to play "Amazing Grace" on the piano. Everyone sang along. As I began, *Amazing grace how sweet the sound that saved a wretch like me. I once was lost*, I froze for about ten seconds, and so did everybody else; they all stopped singing. Then I began again, and everyone joined back in that very moment, *but now I'm found, was blind but now I see*. Talk about funny; we still crack up every time my aunt plays the funeral tape.

I did well working out of our home in my self-employed business, and so did my kids in their skills in piano, ballet, tap, dance, guitar, drums, trombone, baseball, football, basketball, hockey, soccer, skateboarding, snowboarding, surfing, etc., etc., etc. My first big purchase for our family was a baby grand piano for my ten, eleven, and sixteen-year-old children. However, I will confess it was mostly for me to enjoy their beautiful songs being played out gently and softly by their precious little fingertips.

My husband was also very successful in his work and very responsible for paying for all of the necessities in our home, such as the mortgage, utilities, maintenance, and food. I was responsible for taking care of all the fun. So, I would spend my earnings on toys, ski trips and taking them on one-on-one trips with me. We traveled throughout Europe, Nassau, and the Caribbean.

Whether we traveled or were at home, there was nothing more important to me than the gentle comforts I could provide in atmosphere for my family. The atmosphere is so key that I always wanted to surround my family with comfort. I have included some photos of my family at the end of this chapter, starting with Figure 27.

### *Driving Minivan on Golf Course*

I was always en route it seemed, driving the latest and biggest white minivan with my boys in the back. One fine, beautiful, sunshiny day, we were on our way to a birthday party at a swanky country club located on a lovely green golf course. As I was pulling up to find parking, unaware that I took a wrong turn, I found myself driving on the little road for the golf carts.

### *Patrick and John*

My boys were both yelling out at me as they sank onto the floor, "Mom! Oh, my God! Get off!"

I couldn't make a U-turn without the van having to go onto the turf. So, I rode it out, found the entrance, and then dropped them off near their friends. They walked in with their tail between their legs. Our family never lacked in laughter.

I think being gentle with each other brought out the humor for us.

## *Tatum*

With my daughter, it was always her and I and all her friends. Being the little social butterfly with personality plus, she was always bubbly and happy, friendly, and full of passion. She started talking and walking at eight months old, impressively remembering everybody's name. We would be together shopping, and from her seat in the cart at the grocery store she would wave while smiling and greeting everyone. I got her started in tap dance when she was two, the youngest little ballet dancer ever to be trained by Ms. Taylor, the world's best. As a stay-at-home mom working out of our home, I was always available to be there with her and her friends doing girly things.

I loved being the designated hairdresser and taking care of all her friends' hair and makeup. When she went off to college I helped decorate and clean her dorm room.

For her twenty-first birthday our family, along with her best friend, all celebrated together at her favorite restaurant. It was very upscale with white linen tablecloths and fine wine. We had gotten the girls a limo so they could leave after dinner and have a good time. I knew for sure they would go partying, so I called the restaurant beforehand and told them I wanted them to serve us, the girls, my husband and me, non-alcoholic wine.

We all arrived at our reservation as planned and enjoyed our wonderful dinner. As the server was pouring my third glass from the white napkin-covered bottle, my daughter said,

"Mom, take it easy, that's your third glass."

Her little brothers were grinning from ear to ear. As we were finishing our evening together, the girls were anxious to get out and into the limo awaiting them. My daughter's friend said, "Wow, I'm buzzed, thank you so much for dinner. That was the best wine ever."

My daughter's gentle and loving spirit allowed me to make her twenty-first birthday the happiest. I know she appreciated all my efforts of making her atmosphere perfect on her special day. It was my gentle loving SPIRIT in charge.

The boys and I probably waited maybe a couple of weeks to tell her about the fake wine. I couldn't bring myself to giving my daughter alcohol and then sending her out on the town. I wasn't overly strict; I just never really had alcohol in our home when our kids were growing up to not be a temptation for them. This was another one of my dad's good habits that I had chosen to implement and follow in raising my children. Of course, in my mom's home she kept a full bar from which she would happily serve my friends Pink Squirrels and Grasshoppers, her famous drinks.

I have to chuckle at myself as to finally understanding why it is now that I have such a dislike for sweet drinks.

I always took excellent care of my mom. I would take her shopping and loved buying her things and helping her and her husband financially.

Because she grew up in an orphanage after losing her mom at the age of two, I completely understand why she was like she was. I was grateful for my mom because having her was far better than not. She did the best she knew how to do.

I would sometimes catch myself just staring, mesmerized and captivated by my mom's beauty. To me, she was the most beautiful woman in the world. Her hair was so thick and long that she would have it done at the beauty salon weekly. That was one of her good habits that I have taken on, pampering myself weekly in getting my hair done. While traveling throughout the world, I still managed my long head of hair in local beauty salons.

### *Happy Times*

In 2017, I traveled to the City for Peace, Hanoi, Vietnam, where there sat a very special beauty salon/meat market. The hotel staff would kindly walk me through the busy traffic, the two blocks to the salon, intertwining among the people, motorcycles, and cars that would often come within a hair of my body.

Inside, I would comfortably lay on my back on a huge pleather bed with my head over a sink for forty minutes with my hair being gently washed by a young and beautiful Vietnamese woman as her two-year-old baby boy played at the bottom of my feet.

Then I would be in the chair for another hour while she styled my hair, and we exchanged our life stories.

In the back, there was raw meat hanging to be sold by the pound, and underneath in the showcase counter were bras and panties that looked like something my grandmother would wear. Getting my hair done is my thing. I've gotten it done all over the world. I love having my hair washed by somebody else. It's just the gentlest thing I could have done for myself and knowing that I have somebody touching my head, and it's almost a purity with water as I'm cleansed; it sounds weird, but it's true for me.

### *Going Home and Seeing My Family*

I would travel every two months to take care of my dad, assisting with doctors' appointments, surgeries, the organizing of his house, and the preparation of two months of food for his freezer so he would have my home-cooked meals in between my visits.

I'll never forget canceling my dad's back surgery just two days before the procedure. Let's say the hospital was a bit pissed because it was a $60,000 loss for them. I did so after learning that they were going to slice his back wide open and then put him into a turtle shell that he'd have to wear for six months of recovery in a nursing home. That would've killed him, and I knew it.

So, I got busy and searched the internet and found a place called Micro-Spine that performs the procedure with a tiny incision by going in microscopically. Very little downtime in recovery and a cost of $20,000 out-of-pocket made this the optimal choice. So, there I went, off to fly with him to DeFuniak Springs, Florida for his surgery. We stayed at the Marriott Hotel where he would have three days to recuperate very near the hospital. We met some other nice families there who were getting the same procedure done. I developed an immediate friendship with this one gal who was there with her mom and dad. We were all talking and hanging out together, and I'll never forget what she said to me.

"Phew, girl, when you get to heaven your crown is going to be so full and heavy with jewels from what you have had to endure and put up with from that father of yours."

I would describe my dad as a handsome, one-of-a-kind, quirky but strange and hilarious agent from a different planet indeed. However, just like my mom, the one thing my dysfunctional parents share is *moi!*

My dad's surgery was such a success, and he was up and walking the halls soon after and feeling much better.

It is so obvious for me to see now how I slowly, throughout the years, bit by bit, lost myself by taking care of my husband, children, mom, and dad. This care resulted in the unfolding of such beautiful and genuine, personal soul-connections between each of us that's deeply planted and ingrained within me today. For that, I am thankful. As my journey continued, however, I finally began to ask, "What is it that you want, Patricia Ann?" I also wanted to be gentler with other people in my life. I realized that while I'd been focused on gentleness with other people, that I hadn't been very gentle with myself. The way to better take care of those around me was to better take care of myself.

### *My Journey to Freedom*

After this stark realization in 2009, it was like the floodgates opened, and I dove deeply into my newfound freedom. From that very moment, I took on a brand-new world. Within four months, thirty pounds had slowly fallen off me. I began taking classes and getting trained and certified to teach health and wellness. I started eating healthy and being careful about what I put into my body. I started taking care of myself.

My friends and family were amazed at my transformation in becoming the new me. They were a bit shocked at first and clueless of how unhappy I was before as I had always pretended my life was perfect!

It's been quite an adventure finding myself and discovering my identity. It seems like doors just kept opening wider and wider and still are, as I continue to be SPIRIT-led.

When I began to focus on making myself a priority, educating myself, and achieving certifications and degrees just for me, instead of my husband and kids, opportunities began to surface.

I was able to travel to Italy in exchange for teaching a one-hour class per day.

I'll never forget telling my youngest son John, "I'm going to go to Italy, and I'm going to be just like the movie, *Under the Tuscan Sun.*"

He had such a sad look on his face asking, "But, Mom, how are you going to understand the language when you don't speak Italian?"

Although I was only kidding with him about the movie, I stayed for almost a month in Italy. I was hosted by an amazing couple that showed me their beautiful culture; they live in Verona. We explored Florence, Venice, Lake Gupta, and visited their family members high up the mountains. At this time, right after my divorce in 2012, I needed their kind gentleness, and they gave it to me.

### *Deep in the Culture – Never a Tourist*

I went out with their family and friends, maybe ten of us, all sitting around a large table in the basement of a cool authentic pizza restaurant. The only two Americans were my friend's husband and me. I felt like I was in a movie waiting for the Godfather to appear, finding us all hidden down in the basement.

I think the wine may be writing out some of my fantasies because all we did was drink wine and limoncello after each heavenly-divine and delicious meal. I finally had to say no when my friend's brother came at 10:00 a.m. wanting me to join him for a wine tasting.

Another wild and awesome night was when my friends invited me to go to a concert that their good friend was promoting at the Pied Piper, a hot local venue. I was excited, ready to go, and dressed up funky, wearing my cool purple pants. When I walked inside this spectacular building at the top of a mountain, I was totally blown away. The inside was full of lavish u-shaped white leather sofa seats seating a dozen people around each table. Hanging above each table was a grand chandelier. The tablelike booths were facing a huge stage, and the room seated comfortably maybe seven hundred people or more dressed to the nines. There they were serving a seven-course meal, and as I found my seat around the table with my friends, I met their good friend who was performing the concert. He could not speak any

English, but he had heard that I was a dancer and wanted me to participate in a song and dance with him.

Well, not only was I freaking out about this so-called concert, but it was also in one of the most amazingly beautiful places I've ever seen. I was spellbound taking in the breathtaking views from the balconies that overlooked the rolling vineyards and mountains. With my hands waving, I spoke out in my best attempt at an Italian dialect ever, "Look, I only dance solo or maybe exercising and teaching groups of people to this specific music on my iPhone."

He brushed it off and in his thick accent replied, "Ah no, ah just-a-you follow my lead when it a-comes a-time."

Which was by no means spoken in any form of language I was able to understand. I immediately grabbed my glass of champagne and gulped it down. Soon after, he came over to my table with his mic, singing out to me while gently taking my hand and bringing me out on the floor. We danced a full tango, my first tango, complete with an extravagant dip.

Then much to my surprise a roar of applause and a standing ovation. I felt brave, with my kind loving and gentle spirit, which allowed me to go up on stage and trust in a singer and dancer. Then, to top it off, Brian May of Queen was there visiting from London.

We talked, and of course, I got my picture taken with him. By the end of the concert, we, Sami my dance partner, Brian, and the band, were all up on stage singing; don't ask me what!

But oh, what a concert and night for this American girl!

### *The Earth Shook*

It was maybe a week after the concert when I was in a deep sleep around three in the morning and was awakened by my bed, shaking me up into the air. It was so crazy that I was lifted out of my bed and shaken and rattled at the same time.

The next morning when I got up and was ready to do the one-hour fitness class with my friend, I said, "That was some earthquake last night!"

She said, "What earthquake? I didn't feel anything."

"Let's turn on the news," I replied.

She did, yet nothing was being reported. I then thought and said out loud to my friend, "Oh my, I believe God came to me and was trying to talk to me early this morning at three, and I don't remember what he was saying."

Then finally, her husband said, "Yes, there was an earthquake last night, and I felt it too."

I was so relieved yet quite sad as some people lost their lives that day. I felt safe knowing my ever so loving and gentle SPIRIT is always in control of taking care of me wherever in this world I am with earthquakes, hurricanes, sexual predators, sniper shootings, stalkers… my SPIRIT has me covered.

### *Heart to Heart*

I want to give the true meaning of awareness to you out there, reading my words and capturing your heart in connecting to mine. Sharing some of my most personal experiences with my partners, kids, parents, friends, and strangers are facing the truth within myself with love and gentleness. In this I can completely accept myself with no discrimination, judgment and blame from my parents or others.

I want to reveal and uncover my all as I write here on these pages, the good, the bad, and the ugly. I believe full-heartedly that we, and every one of us, are connected by our spirit as one to the universe.

No matter how dark the storm may be inside or out, the light is always there within our reach. It's quite simple; all we must do is be like a tree. In yoga, Tree Pose is standing tall with the four corners of our feet firmly planted into the ground while slowing raising up our arms with our hands in prayer, reaching up, and receiving all that's in our reach.

When I was trying to cover up my true self by overeating, running away, and self-numbing, I wasn't fooling anybody but myself. If I were to tap, tap, tap with my fingers on my own heart and ask myself, "What do you want, Patricia Ann?" there would be nothing. Just an empty hollow void needing constant gratification of food, alcohol, or whatever to feed my endless void.

My true experiences are now in this present moment in telling my story of *My Fight Club Within*. I hope that you'll pause, swallow a bit, and maybe feed upon some of my crazy stories. Perhaps some of my words are tugging on your heartstrings from my journey of gently drawing inward with pure love in comforting my soul. I hope that you'll relate in a manner of understanding and see how, when practiced daily (MFCW), your challenges will become opportunities. With spending every moment, we have in building our own unique personality where we can create our authentic, beautiful self – realizing that nobody can fulfill us, or our own beautiful lives, but ourselves.

I accept myself and am aware that I will continue to fuck up, but not now in this very moment. For I know that I am loved; there is nothing for me to fear and there is nothing I can do wrong. For when I look and reach up to receive love, I make that gentle shift over. It's quite simple just to turn the moment around and allow my SPIRIT to lead.

And, oooooohhhh! What a true feeling it is to shine my light.

Step 1. Awareness – if I feel

Step 2. Action – I can heal

Step 3. Allow – and be real

*This is how I fight my battles.*

**Figure 27: FAMILY**

**Figure 28: FAMILY**

**Figure 29: FAMILY**

**Figure 30: FAMILY**

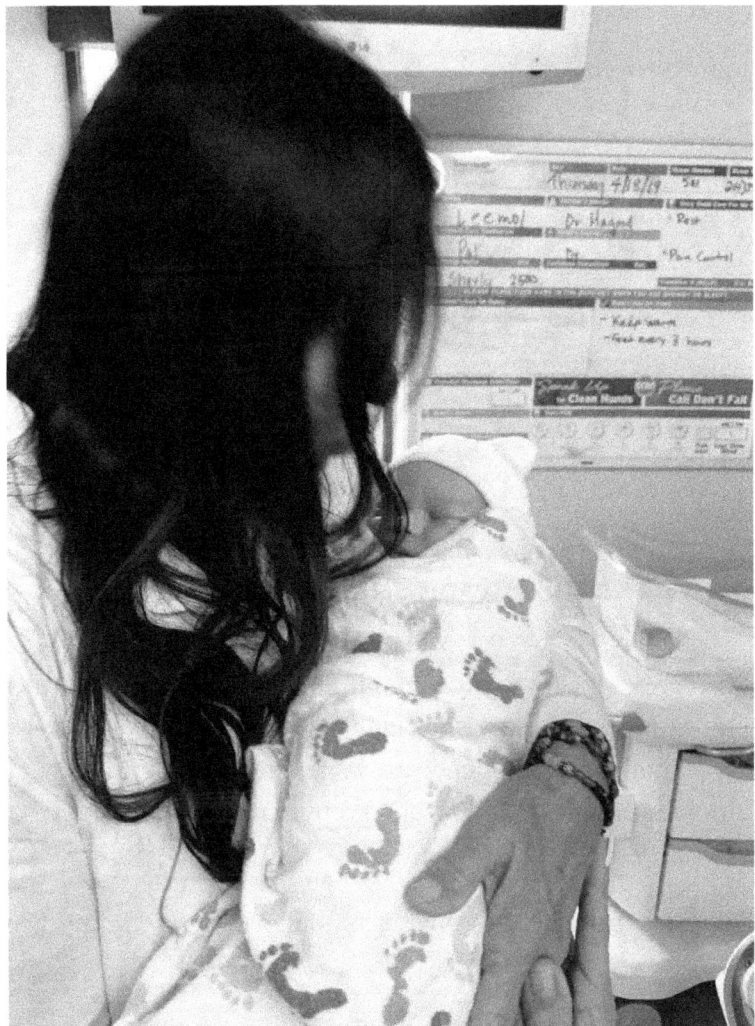

**Figure 31: FAMILY**

# 9. Self-Control

*"Never to suffer would never to have been blessed."*
*~Edgar Allan Poe*

Self-control is keeping my commitment to love. In being true to my commitment, my inner soul radiates out into every move I make. Daily my emotional intelligence grows and matures, but I must always check in with myself first, "What's going on with me? And, what do I need to do?"

Facing my truth first is what sets me free, allowing my Spirit to lead the way.

Indulgence is when my boundaries are poor and weak. I then run away to escape. This continues with me getting stuck in those negative emotions of hate, sorrow, anxiety, frustration, meanness, selfishness, disregard, and harshness all sticking in my body, making me ill.

My spiritual emotions of love, joy, peace, patience, kindness, gentleness, and self-control cover all of me, inside and out, with light.

It is impossible for even the smallest flicker of light to be covered by darkness. Light will always shine through.

Yes, the light is what sets me free, and my wedding reception is the place to be for me. That's where there are dancing and singing and moving to the grooving.

*This is how I fight my battles.*

### *Being One's True Self Attracts Likewise*

Commitment is a big word and is the most important word of all for me in this chapter of self-control. In February 2019, I was talking on the phone to my friend Darla, as I'm about to begin here on this topic of self-control, we shared in a much-needed, especially here on my end, hardcore belly laugh.

It is dang hilarious when it comes to me having control of myself. I tend to jump right in when it comes to pleasuring myself, that is, with healthy and clean fun with my boundaries intact.

### *The Out-of-Control Dating Pool*

After my divorce in 2012, dating for me was intense at first, especially along with having a stalker who followed me everywhere. I had no choice but to go into hiding. So, I spent a lot of time with some of my many cousins and friends who live throughout the United States.

Being with healthy family members who are supportive, loving, and kind is what got me through. Taking me under their wings in creating beautiful memories with my cousins and their amazing, precious kids was just what I needed.

Aware of being followed continuously, I tried to do things differently and out of the norm.

My very first date was a blind date set up by my hometown city friend back on the east coast. She, being a firecracker of a realtor that I found while purchasing one of our many homes with my husband, we became the best of friends, and I would dress her up encouraging her as she was going through a divorce when we first met maybe ten years ago.

I'm kind of famous in my hometown city as you will read a bit later here. She would later tell me how all the guys in her office could not believe that my husband and I were a fit.

My friend now single and knowing a few eligible bachelors, one that she felt we would have a fun time double dating out on the town was now set in motion.

I flew in on a Saturday morning and went shopping at Nordstrom that did my makeup, normally I only wear lipstick, but I went all out for my first blind date as a newly single girls' night out in my hometown.

We had so much fun doing the city and me getting recognition for my former career as a Playboy Bunny.

We danced the night away. When we were done, my new boots had given me the biggest blister on the big toe of my foot. I was so impressed with my date as he lifted me up onto the counter removing my boot to kiss my owie. It was a gross, ugly bleeding and open wound, but oh how sweet he was in making me feel so special.

My blind date has a Harley and almost one year later he had tickets for us to attend the Harley Davidson weekend Rot Rally in Austin, Texas. I was four rows back with Ted Nugent entertaining thousands of peeps. Crowds do a number on me; I get claustrophobic. This rally made Talladega seem tame compared to this with topless tattered up gals proudly riding on the back of their man. I told my date, "No way will I participate and take my top off."

Here he was at this huge bike rally but without his nice bike that was parked far-away at his home. He explained his thoughts and feelings of us being together sharing a hotel room without having sex.

He went on to say, "Patricia, do you see that most beautiful bike up on the pinnacle displayed for the eyes of the beholder? That's how I feel about you. Here you are with me, but I can't have you.

I replied, "I am sorry, but I cannot separate love, sex, and emotions." I went back to the hotel, got my dog, and loaded up the car to make my long drive home. I was proud of myself for showing the self-control to leave the situation.

### *Rhythm and Soul*

My self-control soon would be put to the test. I had the eeriest, creepiest feelings as I was being followed and chased down by an unwanted lurker. I had stopped going out to eat by myself. So, it was nice when my cousin visited for the weekend. He chose a cool restaurant as I was treating him for dinner after leaving his family to come help me out and stay with me.

As our server brought out our delicious entrees, and we were about to take our first bite, there the creep sat at the bar with his back facing me and our table. I turned white as a ghost when my cousin asked, "What's wrong?"

I replied, "He's here. Look behind you." We immediately got our check and food to go.

As I gave up my dining out in public restaurants, I would now have to resort to calling in my food orders to pick up. So, I would have to eat at home alone. One evening, as I went to one of my favorite restaurants to pick up my carryout orders while waiting in the lobby, the creep showed up again. He was coming towards me trying to force me in the corner. I quickly ran through the crowded restaurant back into the kitchen, where the police were called.

The lurker was everywhere. As I would wake up in the morning letting my dog, Cookie, out, there he'd be across the lake peering into my backyard.

I had taken up fitness and dance but had to give that up at my favorite Fitness Center as some of my friends and members would notice him out in the parking lot looking through the windows as I danced.

One of my courses in fitness training was located in a rather seedy section of town. I was on my way within two blocks or so when I came up to a red light and noticed a work boot flying through the air. Then as I looked to my right, I see laying in the crossroad a middle-aged man with the bluest eyes staring directly into mine. He was under the wheels of an SUV, with half of his clothes missing scattered in the street. He wasn't the man who'd been stalking me. Then up ahead on the road directly facing the man were three figures kneeled before him in dark hooded robes.

Now, I think the hooded figures might have been spirits. I can't explain it any other way.

It was as if time stood still, and I was in another world as this man just stared into my eyes; just him and me. I knew he was dead, but his spirit was beaming out like a torch piercing through me and deep within my soul.

I don't recall or know how I even got to the place I was going. But when I arrived, I was hysterically trembling and shaking in shock. My group of Rhythm and Soul Sisters inside came out as I collapsed on the side of the wall trying to tell them what I just witnessed.

Always prepared and ready with an overnight bag in the trunk of my car, I called my cousin right away. I went home and grabbed my dog, then drove three and a half hours nonstop to my cousin's home. My dog, Cookie, and I stayed for well over a month. Sometimes, having self-control means knowing how to take care of yourself. I needed to get away, to recover, and I did just that.

### *Being with Family and Online Dating*

When I was ready to dip my toes back into dating, I joined an online dating service site in the same states where I was in hiding with my cousins and their families.

On my second online-matched date, I met up with a college professor spending over three hours at dinner, receiving my first big lesson on how to date.

After sharing how I had come out of a twenty-three-year marriage, his advice to me was I needed to put myself out there and date many different men to learn about their uniqueness and how I relate to each, discovering along the way what I need. Because I had only been with one man, I needed to explore; I was clueless and had no idea what I was looking for in a man.

He explained and made it clear that I can't sit at home praying to God to send me my Boaz. That most likely, the only knocking on my door will be from the Jehovah's Witness, Mormons, and UPS men.

Thus, dating became a numbers game for me, and I was on a roll. I would sometimes have three dates in one day typically meeting at Barnes & Noble or Starbucks with one of my cousins sitting in the crowd at a table nearby.

I still chuckle as I think back at meeting maybe my third date and watching and hearing my cousin across the room laugh out loud as he looked so much different than his profile pictures.

Number seventeen happened to be a very famous guy. I was an open book with the majority of my dates, telling them what number they were and what my plan was in getting to know all the many different types of men.

This guy was a hoot, number seventeen, really dazzled me with his confidence and fame when he said, "There shall be no number eighteen. I know you will choose me."

We met for lunch one afternoon; he had two younger sons that were seven and eight that he needed to pick up after to take out for pizza.

I got back to my cousin's house, and we're all excited about who I just had a date with when I get a text from him. It read, "I am so addicted to you; please let me come pick you up and take you to have pizza with my sons and me."

I was so disappointed with him. I couldn't believe he wanted me, a strange woman he'd just met, to meet his boys. It didn't feel right for the boys and me. It was a turn-off. It would be a year in a half later that I was up in the triple digits and never having more than three dates with each guy. Although my dating was out of control, I was captivated by learning all that I could about men and their uniqueness.

Three different men that charmed me into six dates, each putting me off the market for six months in a row was a super cool experience for me. My sincere desire and intention to settle down with one emotionally present, quirky gent made especially for me.

So, bachelor number one was a great kisser, very handsome, fit, and kind. I'll call him Sore Lips Guy. My lips were chapped the entire six weeks of dating him. My daughter grew so tired of my complaining about how badly my lips hurt. He reminded me of my high school days of making out while getting dry humped against the side brick wall of the schoolyard building.

The second guy lived in the city, and he was my first six-foot-four metrosexual man wearing skinny designer jeans and not a hair out of place. Metrosexual Man loved taking me to the nicest restaurants, dancing and live music always graciously complimenting me on my appearance. I loved getting his take and advice on how I looked in my latest hair style and outfit.

On one of our dates, I remember him saying to me, "I like you a lot, but I know I will end up saying something to you that I will regret and lose you."

"I replied with, no, you won't. I'll never get mad at you."

One late night, I receive this text from him saying, "Patricia, we have been together now for over six weeks. When are we going to fuck?"

Three was the charmer. He was from my hometown, and he worked creating robots for a living. We met on the dance floor and wowza, did he have the moves. I was fascinated with his quirky style and laid-back personality.

It was rather strange that I had this cough the entire time of dating him as I would not get too close as an excuse in not giving him my cough. Thanksgiving came around, and he was going back east to be with his kids.

He had a beautiful home not too far from me that was on the market for sale. When he returned home after the holiday, he called wanting to see me. He asked about my cough, as I assured him it was gone, and I was all better.

I asked him about his house that sold, and he told me he was going to move back east. I said, "Okay, I don't think it's a good idea for us to be in a relationship if you're moving." I call him the six-week Cough Guy.

Another interesting date was with a fireman who was just a couple of years younger than me. I met him at a Chili's restaurant for lunch. I walked in and saw him in a booth with a six-month-old baby in a car seat next to him. He looked over at me and asked, "Is this a deal-breaker?"

I did everything in my power to control my laughter, but he was dead serious, and I could still see the shock in his eyes and on his face.

His life was clearly out of control. If there were a poster child for the opposite of self-control, he'd be it. He told me his story of how he was dating a nurse who was a bit younger and claimed she was on birth control and didn't want any children.

He already had two older children in their twenties with grandchildren and had been in a long-term marriage. Apparently, he felt tricked and betrayed by her. She was pregnant at the age of forty-five while claiming she was on birth control, and he certainly wasn't going to make that same mistake again.

After the date and being on the phone with my daughter, we laughed hysterically about the date. She was so worried about me being with a guy who had a baby younger than hers. My beautiful granddaughter was eight months at that time.

I have four of the most beautiful and awesome grandchildren that I get to spoil and love on, and a fifth one on the way, due November 2019. There is no greater honor for me than being Nana to Dawson, Ella, Kinsley, and John. Brilliant results take root here with their little great-great-great-grandmother's faithful prayers over me; a labor of love bringing forth the fruits of the SPIRIT.

### *The Three V's – Vagina, Vulnerable, Venturesome*

I guess you could say my vay-jay-jay for me ranks right up there next to God. Being raised by a very strict dad taught me the value of my body.

Kids that have been raised by an alcoholic or drug-addicted parent tend to grow up gravitating towards or against the drug. If they follow in their parent's footsteps, it becomes their primary law of attraction, or even if they don't, it can still dominate and have an unhealthy effect on them.

The same goes for me in growing up with a religious and stern father. As you read on you will understand why at the young age of eleven, I made a promise and commitment to my dad that I would never grow up to be like my mother. Just as a child of an alcoholic parent chooses not to allow that to dominate them and control their life, I decided at a very young age to protect what I felt to be my most sacred part of my body, my vagina.

That awful vision I experienced as a young child of the pedophile in the park made a significant impact on my opinion concerning masturbation.

I feel that if a person can do that act with themselves alone, where is the need for interaction with another human being and where is the love connection? I know this is maybe a touchy subject (smile). So, please don't take offense by any of my personal opinions. This is simply me; no judgment on myself or you.

Seriously, the only time I go down in that area is to wash. After having my last baby, I was very dry and thought I felt there was a little extra skin down there. So, I went in to see the gynecologist explaining to him my concern.

He then took me back in his office while taking out a piece of paper with a pencil and drew a picture of a vagina. He then drew the outer flap while looking up at me and said, "That, my dear, is your clitoris, a much needed and important part." We both busted out laughing.

I can be outrageously silly and goofy at times in my own unique, venturesome way, but at the same time, I want to be transparent and real on these pages. If I had a chance for a do over of my life, I'd keep everything as is. I had purchased the entire series, I was obsessed with *Sex in the City*, watching all their episodes during my separation and divorce. I never watched it on HBO when my kids were home. Then after going to New York and doing the Sex in the City Tour, I discovered the infamous Pink Rabbit on the shelf at the gift store. The Pink Rabbit is one of the most famous vibrators for sale. I laughed so hard thinking back on the episode of Charlotte when she spent hours alone with the Rabbit.

Another funny episode was with Miranda's Nanny snooping in her nightstand finding her vibrator and swapping it out with a statue of Blessed Mary.

So, I will admit that after being single and alone for over a year and a half that I went out secretly to a sex shop and bought the pink or purple rabbit and batteries, spending over one hundred dollars, but I could not bring myself to using it or trying it out. So, after having it for maybe a couple months hidden in the back of my closet still in the bag with the receipt, I tried to take it back. Talk about a laughing matter, when they explained that they couldn't take it as a return because it's unsanitary. I didn't even think about that, and that made it even all the nastier to me. I finally just took the bag with the receipt in the box and threw it down a dumpster and never gave thought to it again, until just now. That's been the closest for me with masturbation.

### *The Three D's – Drinks, Dinner, Dancing*

I decided to move to Paradise back in 2015. At the time, I was working fast paced and nonstop in a big city, being caught up in the so-called rat race of life and trying to avoid the pain from the loss of my mother earlier in the year.

My day would start with waking up, getting to the fitness center for 8:30 a.m. class, and then onto being on my feet for my full-time job in sales by 10:00 a.m. That would end at seven. Then off to meet my friends for the three D's – drinks, dinner and dancing and maybe getting back home and to bed by midnight. The next day I'd do it all over again.

This went on until October of 2015 when I tripped and fell over a construction hose in my building, causing me to break my right big toe.

### *Couch Potato Period 10/15/2015 thru 2/2017*

That was the most horrendous and nightmarish thing that could have happened to me. My life stopped completely, resulting with me laid out flat on my back having to use crutches when I walked, resulting in being caged inside my deluxe high-rise in the heart of downtown.

All the activities that I lived and loved to do – exercising, dancing, walking, hiking, running, and working were now all gone.

I got caught up inside the tunnel tube of Netflix, documentaries, and movies. Being single after surgery in a big, ugly, black boot all doing the Christmas and New Year's holidays was not at all a good fit and look on me. I sank into a deep depression in feeling sorry for myself. But, with much prayer, and with the support, kindness, and love of my good friends Iris, Susy, Faith, Brooke, Marla, Randy, Billy, Holly, Regina, and Tisa, I made it through remarkably well. I was equipped with all my beautiful friends' wisdom and encouragement, cheering me upward and onward to my new life and big move to somewhere in Paradise.

Sometimes we get so busy existing in our world of chaos that is out-of-control that we become unaware of how dysfunctional our behavior is driven by stuff to do and to be done.

Honestly, I would make fun of myself first in saying how I know I have issues, and all my dysfunctional friends having their drama and issues mixed with mine was a lethal cocktail for disaster. As much as I know that they all love me and didn't want to see me leave, they understood that I had to go and follow my heart.

Breaking my right big toe was the most debilitating disastrous dilemma for this extreme, highly energetic, active gal to be in.

I now look back and see it as one of the greatest blessings and best thing that could have ever happened to me, bringing that life to a complete halt, and taking me off my feet.

I had no choice but to lay down, relaxing my overly worked BODY. I stopped ignoring and began spending time with my sweet little CHILD. I gave heed to my positive thoughts in caring for my ADULT brain making some healthy and lifechanging decisions for me.

Once again, I heard the voice of my SPIRIT softly speaking out to me, "Patricia Ann, it is time for you to wake up now."

I knew I needed to move. I planned that I would recover from my surgery and I would move forward. I felt closed in living in the desert and wanted to get out and breathe and see the world and be by the water. They were desires within me that I didn't realize I had.

### *Too Much Time on My Hands*

Going from always on the go to completely still and off my feet, was the worst situation for me to be in. Before my accident, in my place, I would spend no more than five, six hours a night solely for sleep and a shower.

One of my last two dates, before breaking my toe, was with a pastor who led a vast congregation in another state that I had met online. He had taken me out to dinner and then dancing, as my thoughts wandered on in seeing myself as a pastor's wife.

Laugh, I don't think so. I was fascinated with him and enthralled deeply in conversations listening to his stories. I loved how he had such self-control.

He told me of how his brother had met a beautiful woman who had been obese, and after having bariatric surgery, she then had a total bodyweight lift. He said it was remarkable.

Back at home with broken big toe laid out permanently on my sofa, I began looking at myself so closely at all my flaws; especially of the little extra flab on my arms and legs. Thinking about what that pastor had said about the amazing results, and I had to have surgery anyway, on my toe. I could now recover at the same time in making my body even better.

I am such a planner. I began to seek out and find doctors to perform my surgery. I got many "No's." I've never been more than forty-five pounds overweight in my entire life; until one day, one said, "Yes."

Realizing this was absurd, what I was about to do to myself, I had to keep this totally to myself. However, I had to tell at least one person to have someone to drive me and stay with me the night after my surgeries. Yes, I got arms and legs done at the same time resulting in an all-day surgery.

And, yes, my friend did try to talk me off the ledge, but I am very persuasive once I make my mind up to do something.

I didn't get the results and had to get another corrective surgery, but this time with a surgeon who knew what he was doing in correcting me.

There is no explanation I can give to you at this moment as to why I hurt myself or set myself up under the knife. My only hope now as you continue in reading *My Fight Club Within*, that you will have a better understanding of me being a past cutter.

In February 2019, after six months on my own and after the break-up of my relationship, I feel it's time for me to start dating.

What I miss most from my being with and in love with my boyfriend, is his gentle touch. When we were together, we were bonded with constant physical touch, we totally connected. I've only received hugs from strangers and my newfound friends here in paradise.

### *Am I Ready for Dating?*

In March 2019, I met someone that I feel is a good man. Having had now six dates with him, I feel myself slowly opening, allowing him in.

My heart is guarded, but still, I realize it is always my responsibility to keep my heart open. I know it is as important to receive love as it is to give. It is easy for me to offer, but I am struggling with receiving now.

This is a huge challenge for me because I've only had a couple of short-term relationships since my divorce. The good thing is that each one has been far greater and healthier than the last. I feel like I'm back now to the beginning, so I want to learn from the past and apply my newfound discoveries.

It's fun chatting with my boss, Sara, about my latest dates with my new guy. I'll call him Good Man. I find myself regularly standing there explaining how wonderfully generous and kind he is to me. On our last date on St. Paddy's Day, while sitting on a park bench having an intellectually optimistic conversation, we observe a little girl and boy flying a kite. The kite gets stuck in a tree, and my six-foot-four guy softly excuses himself as he goes off in his dad-mode to free the kite for the children. Sara responds with, "Aww, how sweet. He's a keeper, girl."

Then I say in return, "But he's just so nice, kind and good to me that it's scaring me."

Sara replied, "Why are you acting like a twelve-year-old, Patricia? Still wanting to be with the bad boys? You should be more mature and acting your age, having a good man to spend the rest of your life with. Why on earth would you want to waste any of your time with a dickhead?" I love my friends.

On our first date, the Good Man and I met at a sushi restaurant after my day of work at the Children's Hospital. He was patiently waiting for me in a booth in a dark corner with a blaring light overhead. I sat across from him, facing the wall. As I sat talking with him with the lights glaring in my eyes, I just wanted to move. I said, "You know I'm uncomfortable here in this dark corner. Atmosphere is so important to me. Do you mind if we move up to the sushi bar?"

His response was, "Oh my gosh, yes, of course. Let's move." We were now seated on a comfy stool with the sushi bar in front of us and in the background was a full array of happy people enjoying each other.

I asked him several important questions. "How long have you been single, and what happened in your last relationship to cause it to end?"

He responded, "It's been a year and a half since my last relationship. It ended with her, and her five-year-old moving long distance to another state."

I shared just a little about me, especially that I am a writer and deep into my work in my first book, *My Fight Club Within*. He was very receptive, kind, and laid back in asking me about my writing. I froze and apologized that I am not ready to share. We continued enjoying our sushi together and winding down our date. I took my phone out to call on an Uber. He then offered to drive me home. Of course, I was reluctant and said no, thank you, as I had just met him.

He then did something that took me off guard with being surprised. He pulled out his driver's license and said, "Take a picture and send it to your friend."

I sent it to Darla, and he drove me home in his cool Jeep dropping me safely off at my door.

## *Second Date*

On our second date, he came to pick me up at my place, at the same outside door to my building that he had dropped me off at from on our first date. He was taking me to a live music street festival happening in the downtown area. I made it clear to him that I would not drink more than two drinks and I need to be home by nine o'clock. I had to open up the Castle at 6:00 a.m. the next morning.

## *Nice Having a Man to Talk Car Shop With*

We walked the streets holding hands, his hands were warm, and it felt good embracing the touch that I've been missing. I was Chatty Cathy in talking about my car drama and my issues with having a key programmed.

I had gotten my key wet and replacing it had cost me over five hundred dollars. I miss my dealership; that was my happiest and most favorite service department that was like my family back home. This new dealership is far from paradise, and it takes me forty-five minutes to arrive, and customer service is non-existent. Even though it looks and is set up in the same manner as my old one, the atmosphere is dead. Here it is a Saturday afternoon around 2:00 p.m. and I'm driving there after work to get my key repaired for the second time. There is absolutely nobody in sight as I walked inside this huge, beautiful dealership.

A friendly salesman approaches me as I ask to see a service person and get my oil topped off. He begins apologizing that the service department closes at one o'clock on Saturdays and there was no way for him to get some oil because everything is locked up.

I was surprised but sat down with him as he wrote a huge Post-It note to give to the service department first thing Monday morning. I told him how my key does not fit, and I feel that they may have cut the key wrong. He assured me that that was probably correct and that they would come first thing Monday morning to bring me a car and take mine in to fix this matter.

Monday morning comes, and once again, I wait for a call that never comes. After getting off work again, I call and finally talk to a service person. They tell me they are sure that it is not the key, that it's most likely my ignition that needs replacing, and I will have to bring the car back myself and wait on it.

On my way, I see a place that works on foreign cars, and I run in and tell them my key story. The serviceman was very kind in putting my car on the computer and not charging me the ninety-nine dollars to see if it was my ignition at fault, or a bad key cut. Twenty minutes later, the results arrived. My ignition is good, but my key is bad. I am also in need of new rear brakes replaced, so I get a price for that. I am now back on my way to the dealership with full knowledge that the key is bad. I pull up, and the service guy comes out as I proceed to tell him I know for sure the key is bad. He takes my key and starts my car and says, no, the key is fine, let me take it back and then I will show you that it's most likely your ignition.

I am now arguing back with him in saying look, I took it to a professional expert on foreign cars, and he will even talk to you about the real problem being a bad key cut. He then argues back, "I'm not going to talk to anybody outside about this matter."

I then even bring up the nice salesman who wrote out a detailed note agreeing that it's likely a bad key cut. He then argues back that the salesman has no business advising on a matter of the service department.

At that point, I'm running inside to find the nice salesman while demanding to speak to the service department manager. The service manager comes out and tells me that he too is sure that it is not a bad key and that never once in his twenty years of service had he ever experienced a bad key cut.

By now, I find the nice salesman and sit down with him at his desk filling him in on what's happening. I tell him all about my wonderful dealership back home and how every time I pull in there is a happy-faced greeter opening my car door. It is full of happy people with happy music playing. There is even a tiny bird as a pet that the serviceman feeds cookie crumbs to and the little bird follows him around all day at work.

My service manager back home always asks me how I'm doing and shows interest in my travels and what I've been up to lately. Saturday is their busiest day, with their doors open till seven o'clock at night.

I look at the nice salesman and say, "Look around. There are no happy people, no music, and no love. There is no service.

Never have my calls been returned. Although I've received two calls two different times for verification of appointments for brakes that I never agreed upon or set up. This place is that desperate. How do you make any money? Why would I want to come here and buy a car?"

He said, "I am going to talk to the general manager personally about this matter."

Then, out walks the service manager with his tail between his legs, who says, "Well, I know I said in all my twenty years this has never happened, but you are the first. I will order another key, and have you come back in a couple of days."

Two days later, once again, I am making the three-hour-plus round-trip drive back to the dealership to get my key and waiting for another hour only to have the service manager tell me that it's another bad key.

He claims he will set up another appointment with me bringing my car back and waiting while he takes my key to a local locksmith down the street to see if he can make some minor adjustments to fix the key.

Well, I thought that was the most ridiculously absurd thing to suggest taking my high-tech computerized VIN-programed key that he has already charged me over five hundred dollars to a local locksmith. WTF. Why didn't I think of that and spend maybe fifty-some cents with the Home Depot key making service?

Once again, I find the nice salesman, and I confess that I am livid and beyond being so pissed off in the moment that I feel steam coming out of my head. I leave by saying I don't know what I am going to do. I go into my ring with my team huddled all together in one accord breathing slowly and waiting patiently for my SPIRIT to handle this crazy and crucial out-of-control matter.

I call up my long-distance, happy, and friendly service manager, David, and ask for advice on what to do. It was nearly five o'clock here, closing time, and I hadn't heard back from the local service manager. David said to maybe pray about it and wait till tomorrow. "If you don't hear from him by then, call the general manager."

The next morning, I got a call from the service manager with a whole different attitude. He said he would send my key out to another place that is in California to make another key and bring me a rental car as he would be picking mine up. I ask what he would charge to do my brakes if he would match the price of the other, and he agreed to do so.

My date beautifully listened with intent to my out-of-control dilemma. It was a great second date.

### *Third Date*

On the third date, he took me to the museum that I had wanted to visit. We slowly observed taking in all the beautiful art, strolling through the galleries hand-in-hand.

By now, I had asked him so many questions that felt I knew a bit more about him; after all, I did have his driver's license.

He has an awesome job that he is happy with and is the CEO of the company. He is also a Reiki Master and practices on the side. He loves music and plays the drums and guitar. He owns two homes, one in the city and one just a few miles down the road from me that he is renovating himself.

I feel we are compatible and both on the same page as far as the importance of loving ourselves first. However, I still have some questions that need to be answered in finding out his true intentions towards me. I will find out these answers on our fourth date, which will be on his turf for dinner prepared by him.

### *Fourth Date*

He offered to pick me up, but I decided I wanted to drive myself so that I would behave and not drink too much wine with dinner. I was very impressed with his renovation and by all of his hard work inside and out. I admired the herb garden he was building outside as he heated the grill to cook our dinner.

Inside I felt such a warm ambiance as he proudly showed me all his rooms and then welcoming me into his kitchen with newly installed cabinets and an amazing cooktop stove. He welcomed me with any of my ideas regarding his many tasks at hand.

After dinner, we had our second glass of wine seated comfortably side-by-side on his large leather sofa. He took my hand and said, "Look, I promise I will not rush you; I understand you're wanting to take this slow, but I'd like for you to feel free to talk to me about anything. No pressure, Patricia, okay?"

I wasn't ready to open just yet with my questions. So, I finished my glass of wine and told him I needed to leave.

Barefooted, he walked me out to my car parked in his circular driveway. Opening my car door, he asked me to text him once safely home. Then he proceeded to run out to the street, pointing out to me the direction I needed to travel to head home.

As I drove away, I was experiencing panic and fear of what just transpired. I couldn't get away fast enough in getting home to call my friend Darla.

### *I Was Inside the Dark Ring Again*

I didn't bother to text him, and two hours later, I received his text asking me if I made it home? I replied, "Yes, and thank you so much for the lovely dinner."

I didn't think I'd hear from him again, but two days later, I get a text from him asking me if I'd like him to pick me up and take me out to dinner at our favorite sushi place.

I replied with my most easy and used four-letter word, "Sure."

### *Fifth Date*

On our fifth date, I was fully prepared to let go of the ghost of my past and see him clearly through and with eyes of love. I would be emotionally mature in opening my heart.

However, I wanted to ask those hard questions and be ready for the answers. Tonight, I was prepared to ask the age question. I look remarkably young for my age. When my daughter and I are out together, people always think that we are sisters. Not too long ago when she had her baby girl, and I was with her, the nurses all thought I was her sister, and when she introduces me as her mother most people are just shocked.

When I'm with my sons, separately and even with us three together, we get taken as being a couple. It annoys them when guys that are younger than them flirt and hit on me in their presence.

Don't get me wrong here, I am in no means a cougar or do I want to be. It is a big, big turn-off for me. However, my rule of thumb is that I will not go more than seven years younger.

So back to my date. As I looked over at him while eating our edamame and sipping wine, I mention the fact that I have three grandkids and two are older than your ex's five-year-old.

If you're attracted to younger women than you must realize that I'm not your girl.

He answered me back with something like this, "Patricia, I see you for who you are on the inside. Age is but a number, and you are so much more than that. You are awesome and amazing."

I now feel comfortable enough to let him read the introduction to *My Fight Club Within*. This was the text that I received soon after. "I am home now. Thanks for an awesome introduction to an amazing person and thank you for being you. Goodnight!"

### *Sixth Date*

St Paddy's Day marked our sixth date; we attended a huge celebration by the water, which was the best yet as we shared in many conversations about our family history. It was a full day of celebrating and dancing in the streets to live music.

### *Need to Put the Brakes on Dating*

However, I am still healing and experiencing all these feelings from my broken heart from my last relationship with the Aussie. So honestly, I still really don't know what happened between us except that we were together every moment of the day for days and months in a row. In our entire life, neither one of us had ever been with somebody, our parents, spouse, and kids, for such a long period in time. We were extremely high energy, connected and linked together as one.

True healing happens when I permit myself to feel whatever feelings that randomly pop up from past triggers.

So just like at the beginning of my being here in paradise in my little place on the water, it's as if I'm on a boat surrounded by nature and water. I was so fascinated in the first days with my views in October 2018, taking pictures and video clips while watching the dolphins and manatees and even killer whales out from my walls of windows.

However, now it's as if I hardly look anymore. Why? Is it because my interest has gone to new and better things with seeing bigger dolphins and bigger fish out there?

I don't feel that is the case with the work that I'm doing, living and breathing, right now on these pages of *My Fight Club Within*. I am deeply dedicated, committed, and devoted to love.

I feel that if you have a good thing, and it's there at your disposal 24/7 if you don't care for, appreciate, and nurture it, you begin to take it for granted, and then you lose it.

I am so proud of myself and how I have demonstrated self-restraint by not going back to my ex-boyfriend. I'm staying true to myself with loving self-control and internal discipline.

I will go down in his history as being his greatest loss.

*This is how I fight my battles.*

# 10. Catastrophizing

So, let's talk about *catastrophizing*. And yes, we all do it. During the *Hoffman Process*, I learned that I do this all the time. Remember, we are all human beings, and we all suffer. Let me give you an example of mine and how crazy one Sunday afternoon can be for me.

### *First Visit Home from Paradise*

I'm about to travel for the Christmas holidays in December 2018 to be with family and friends. It's Sunday, and I'm (ADULT) leaving in two days on a Tuesday for a flight out.

I'm feeling a little tickle in my throat (BODY) and feeling a little warm, thinking I may have a fever. Then I feel a slight discomfort in my tummy, so my thoughts (CHILD) begin centering around how sick I was with salmonella in Mexico one year ago. I'm in a new state that possibly won't honor my health insurance. Thinking I'd better nip this in the bud, I start at Walgreens and proceed to spend seventy-five dollars to talk to a staff nurse. I hoped she could quickly take my temperature and check my blood to make sure I don't have some looming bacterial infection. My thoughts then go to, "I have to get this done because I cannot even imagine flying and increasing my illness from maybe a small cough to bronchitis or who knows. I certainly cannot go there and make my family sick."

The nurse is very kind and friendly and understands my situation. She takes my temperature, and I don't have a fever. She explains that she cannot get my blood work done because the lab is not open. She was kind enough to call another clinic who does have a lab and takes my insurance. I get into my car, and I drive to this new place. I have to go to the restroom, but with thinking this clinic may need to take a urine sample, I held off. I went in and filled out all my paperwork, and they agree certainly I could give them a sample. I returned to the desk with my urine sample only to find out that after all that time I spent filling out all the paperwork, they don't accept my insurance, and it would cost me one hundred dollars.

The receptionist then explains that there is another clinic that closes in ten minutes down the road and maybe less in cost for me. They called and confirmed that they do take my insurance, so I asked them if I could take my sample with me so that they'll have it and they said, "Yes."

I throw it in my purse and head down the road. Right before going inside, I noticed that my pee had spilled all over inside my very expensive and most favorite Italian bag. However, even worse yet it's also all over my little paper insurance card. I ran inside, wrapping paper towels around my purse hoping it's not noticed, and I proceed to the counter where they asked for my insurance card. Yep, I handed it to them dripping wet and just gave her an awkward look like don't even say a word. So, they run my card and quite frankly I was so relieved when they said they didn't take my insurance. So, I just replied thank you very much, but I'm gonna go back to the other place because they have all my info and I'll pay a hundred bucks, which I did.

On the outside, I was wearing my mask of a smooth, calm demeanor. Inside, with each mounting affront, my panic deepened.

Absolutely nothing was wrong, except that I was creating chaos within myself.

Yes, I was stuck in my funk, and all I could think about was escaping myself. However, no matter where I go, I am there with myself. So, I must admit that I was pretty darn sick and tired of myself that day. I mean, I literally could not stand myself, that's how bad it was. That is the definition of me catastrophizing. That was when I knew I needed to make some phone calls; I needed help.

### *Sundays*

Sundays are and seem too often to play out as a rather eventful and special day, standing out for me. A large majority of my unique experiences and events tend to fall on that day. A day that is agreed upon by a big part of our universe to be used for maybe rest or to do as we please.

SPIRIT, however, is timeless, naturally dwelling within my body. There is no such thing as time off for a lazy Sunday afternoon for my SPIRIT!

I am fascinated with the human mind and how it works, always connecting one thought to something else, to something else, etc., etc., etc. My string of thoughts involving my CHILD and BODY while catastrophizing creates a heavy negative fog that sticks to my actual body parts, especially in my throat and tummy. So, the fact that my head (ADULT ego) probably weighs about ten pounds – oh my!

By catching myself and identifying these body sensations and experiencing them, I can begin my transformative steps:

Step 1. Awareness – if I feel

Step 2. Action – I can heal

Step 3. Allow – and be real

Progress rests solely upon my willingness to face my truth.

The moment I begin to switch my negative thoughts to the positive, immediately the good and bad things get better, as light fills my body, clearing out the heavy fog. My SPIRIT of super endless and timeless power covers all within my body with light.

Healing begins.

*This is how I fight my battles.*

It appears my whole life has been filled with me catastrophizing; I found myself simply existing and making it through to the next catastrophe.

## *Confessions*

I was always in trouble growing up. Ruminating on impending punishments were normal, everyday thoughts. "Just wait till I get home, my dad's gonna kill me."

I found my dad to be most happy when we would go to our weekly confession. I'd go in and tell the priest about all the stupid shit I'd done. Inside the church I'd enter a small, dark, closet like room and the priest would slide open a little screened window. I would then begin to speak ever so softly, usually with something like this, "Bless me, Father, for I have sinned, it has been one week since my last confession."

"And what is it you are seeking forgiveness for, my child?"

I would then proceed to dish out my weekly misgivings, "My friend and I snuck into the nun's convent; it was my idea because of my curiosity. I wanted to see where Mother Superior and Sister Karen slept at night, what their rooms looked like and if they used a hairbrush because I never get to see the hair hidden under their habit. So, my friend and I hid underneath their beds yesterday, got tired of waiting and then left. Tuesday evening, I jumped out of my bedroom window after my dad thought I went to bed. I turned my fan on because it makes a loud noise. I threw my shoes, belt and my purse on the grass and then wobbled out of the window landing on top of the trashcan that I had earlier placed directly under my window. After my escape, I was off to the carnival to hang out with my friends.

"Last Sunday, my mom's boyfriend picked me up from my dad's. My cousin, Chip, is in town visiting and they brought me to my brother's reception. He was stopping at some bars on the way to get a drink, giving my cousin and me quarters to play the slot machines. Then he asked me if I wanted to drive, three times I declined. And then finally I said, 'Okay, yes.' So, I'm driving for a while, and I got the brake pedal mixed up with the accelerator and crashed through the fence into a side of the house. A pregnant woman came out the door. Nobody got hurt, but we were late making it to the reception, arriving in a tow truck. My mom was furious with me in the bathroom fixing my hair and putting my pretty new dress on me for the party. I can't tell my dad because he will kill me. I must go to court about that even though I only just turned fourteen years old. I hope they don't send me to jail because I didn't want to drive."

Then the priest gave me my penance of several "Our Fathers" and "Hail Marys". I was a busy girl!

I had occasion to revisit the priest not long after. I told him, "Bless me, Father, for I have sinned, it has been one week since my last confession. My cousin, Debbie, was visiting, and we were staying at my mom's for the weekend. I love hanging out with my next-door neighbors. They're older teenagers than me, Diane, and Donna. I decided that Debbie and I would go and sneak into their house and wake them up and get them to come out and play. So, as we go inside creeping ever so lightly up the steps to go into their bedroom, my cousin freaks out and runs out of the house slamming the front door. Their dad wakes up, gets his gun, and comes into their bedroom. I got in between their beds and held my breath because I thought he was going to shoot me. After I heard him go downstairs, I whisper, girls please wake up, your dad is about to shoot me. They didn't."

I always felt better after confession. I am no longer a Catholic, but my faith is what kept me strong in getting me through my chaotic life.

As it turned out, when I had to go to court with my mom's boyfriend, my prayers were answered because as I sat in front of the judge, I didn't have to say a word. I just got to listen as he screamed out at John, "Why would you let a fourteen-year-old girl drive your car?"

I was so embarrassed that I just bent over and pretended to tie my shoes almost the entire time. Of course, I'm still living to tell the story of not getting shot from breaking and entering my neighbor's house. In fact, their mom was laughing so hard that she begged me to allow her to tell her husband that it was me hiding in between the girls' beds. I finally agreed. He sat me up on his lap and said, "Patty, don't ever do that again. If you would have just yelled out to me Uncle Carl, I would never ever hurt you, honey, you're like my child and part of our family."

## *Jealousy*

Jealousy is a touchy subject for me. When I was traveling with my Aussie boyfriend, I knew he wasn't over his ex because I felt her presence. Starting in Bali, I was beginning to feel uncomfortable in that I made a mistake in meeting him there, and I even told him. So, I made sure to pay half, my own way, and not rely on him for money, but I wanted to see the world. So, I relied on him as my guide and told him that I am here, so let's make the best of it. We were already getting closer to the USA, and I felt I should hang in there for just a few more weeks to experience Mexico.

I began to flirt since I wasn't at all going to compete with an ex that he claimed to hate; I still sensed her aura invading my space. Sitting between my boyfriend and a young man to the right, I struck up a conversation with the young man. He told me his age of forty-four and said he was sure to be too old for me because I looked to be about thirty-eight. I laughed and looked over to tell my boyfriend. Then we proceeded to have our first fight. It went on through the night, resulting in the start of the most powerful connection where our romance would begin.

I admitted to my flirting as I could see the pain it caused by the tears in his eyes. In return, he let me know it was three and a half months, not years, since the breakup with his ex. I understood totally at that point and would never flirt again with another. We became closer than ever because we had that honest conversation, and we realized just how much we cared about each other.

Mexico would turn out to be my most favorite place in the world. The people are so joyful, happy, and generous in sharing their hearts, loving their families, working hard, and playing together, enjoying life at the moment. I fell in love with their charming kept history of fine art, music, and architectural beauty displayed and hidden inside town after town.

### *Childhood Memories*

I don't have many memories as a five-year-old, but one that I can still picture in my head stands out. I watched my mom kiss this man out in front of our home. As I stood out in the front yard observing her standing up on her tiptoes leaning into the passenger window of a cement truck, I thought to myself, "Why is my mommy kissing that man and he is not my daddy?" It would be years later when I was in my thirties, that while visiting my dad, he brought out a tape recorder and said, "I want you to hear this."

He played a recording of a telephone conversation with the sad and weepy voice of a man confessing his deepest apologies. The man on the phone explained that years ago while pouring the concrete for our driveway he had an affair with my mom and was asking my dad's forgiveness. He claimed he had become a better man by choosing to be true to himself and not living in guilt. My dad forgave him, but did he ever forgive my mom?

Talk about a blast from the past as I sat there on the porch with my teary-eyed dad on a sunny day gazing out into the front yard – the same yard where I was witness to this horrific act. Both of those men became my heroes that day because that was the strongest and most courageous act of love: to forgive.

I remember how sad my dad was and how I would never want to make somebody feel that way. From a very young age, I set the bar for myself to never repeat my mom's mistakes. It's like self-learning for me by other people's mistakes.

It just seems like there was always a catastrophe happening in my life, but I am still aware and working hard to change now as I reflect on my past.

Forgiveness is key in moving forward.

### *There is Nothing Sexier Than my Authentic Truth*

My SPIRIT is jealous and weeps for me when I dwell in a lack of forgiveness toward myself and others. I am only eroded when holding on to the self-deception that I don't deserve to be loved or happy or that I'm not worthy of living a life free of guilt because of bad things I may do or have done.

My SPIRIT is jealous regarding me and doesn't want me to harbor the insecurities of feeling that I'm not bright enough because I have dyslexia or that I'm not worthy enough to be forgiven.

My SPIRIT will not compete with living in the foolishness of self-sabotage or self-mutilation. I'm finally getting that as I realize that writing this book will go down in history as being my most significant accomplishment of truly freeing myself.

Healing begins here with total commitment inside my ring, *My Fight Club Within*. I am aware that forgiveness to myself is my key ingredient in giving me the strength and courage to write this book.

You and I have a legacy to leave our generations to come with a deep knowing and acceptance of pure SELF-LOVE. The ability to give and receive that love effortlessly is a gift unmatchable.

I'm healing, and I am not alone. I commit under truth and forgiveness daily that I will no longer cause my SPIRIT the pain of jealousy; my secrets are no more.

I'm confident to rest fully assured in trusting myself as being incredibly brave and that I will someday be loved and equally yoked with a real man who believes in himself and has the same values.

### *Back to My Hood, the Castle*

I love romantic and happy movies. I tend to watch my same favorites over and over again. I find myself recreating and implementing some of my favorite scenes from *Maid in Manhattan* with Jennifer Lopez. I love the scene when they're all in their dressing room doing their dance scene. So, when I'm at work in the Castle, I find myself videotaping Sara, my supervisor, whom I feel is one of the best dancers I know. I am under her wing in constant training to teach classes for the guests and members.

### *My Job in Paradise*

I love it when I open the Castle fitness club early in the morning. I have a five-minute walk in the dark, moving briskly with my pepper spray in hand. I love walking in the door through security and through the rustic and old halls containing the employee's kitchen and the massive laundry room where all the sheets, linens, and towels get washed. I swing open the doors to a life full of song, beauty, and grace. Happy jazz music plays in the background as I breathe in the beautiful aroma of fresh flowers, unlocking, and opening the fitness club to begin its day.

I turn on the coffee and bring out the fresh fruit, making sure the locker rooms are well lit and equipped with rolled towels all neatly in place. I walk up through the mystical halls and around the staircase to the lobby, grabbing three sets of *The New York Times, The Washington Post*, and the local paper, to place in my beautiful club waiting room in anticipation for all the happy members and guests to arrive.

I wear a special uniform of shorts and a Polo as I proudly roll the huge cart of dirty towels down the beautiful hallway. Although noticed but seen as a servant to the guests, in my mind, I am the star, playing in my movie *Maid in the Castle*. My cast is my co-workers, like family to me now, as we embrace and dance our new moves just like Jenifer Lopez.

It was 6:30 a.m. when a young lady approached me, asking if I have a broom that she can borrow to clean up some sand she brought into the studio. I smile and reply, "No worries, let me sweep this up."

I could tell she wanted to chat with me, and I felt happy to have some easy morning conversation as well. She asked me if I had ever seen a ghost here in the Castle. I replied, "No, but I have sensed and felt their presence. My observation has been that they are friendly, and I have not experienced any fear of unseen spirits that may be lurking." Then I went back to my work and could not wait to grab the ice bucket going up the old back stairs, a shortcut to the kitchen. That is where Sara said she had seen or felt a ghost, and I am absolutely obsessed with that original old staircase and the heavy demeanor pervading with an air filled with a mysterious old smell that I can't explain.

Sara was among the first friends made in paradise and has no idea of the impact she has made and continues to make on me. Her passion is so addictive when I am around her; I automatically find myself becoming a better me. All it takes is just one look, and she brings an immediate halt to my *catastrophizing*. She is teaching me how to assert with authority my full being, embracing my life.

I am now creating a new and better word to replace *catastrophizing* – *assertivetrophizing*.

Oh, what amazing fun and laughter we share when we lay down on the floor, and I get to be my silly and goofy true self. There is no prejudice in the Castle behind the club desk as we practice some of our exotic moves, replacing all the chaotic thoughts of my past dark uglies.

The laughter we share around me and my present dating reminds me of another one of my favorite movies, *Something's Gotta Give* with Diane Keaton, Jack Nicholson, and Keanu Reeves. In it, Jack Nicholson wanted younger women while Keanu Reeves wanted older women and there was Diane Keaton right in the middle. I feel a kinship with Diane Keaton in that movie. Younger men are sometimes attracted to me, but I am no cougar!

### *What I Want and Don't Want in a Man*

I do desire to share my love in spending this last chapter of my life with a man. I have always adored the three magical park bench scenes in *Kate and Leopold, Leap Year*, and *Notting Hill*, and, yes, I have experienced them by recreating them in my past best relationships and hope to do so again. However, I am also aware that I must continue holding on to my commitment and vows in marriage to myself first.

This Castle is a place of healing, filled with the people who are my family, where I now know I belong. This is priceless. There is no amount of money that could ever buy these amazing moments that are freely given and received directly through the heart.

I finally understand now why I tend to attract intelligent and wealthy men with them spending time trying to impress me.

I think back in time to a third and final date with a pilot, playing Top Golf, when the guy threw his black metal credit card at my feet asking me to pick it up and if I realized what that meant. Another time on a second and last date with a doctor, who took me to a church in his new million-dollar McLaren car. Then a business tycoon, one who never made it to a third date although he was going to fly me in on his private jet to his private island in Hawaii. I blew him off choosing the Aussie instead.

I'm turned off and repulsed by men who try to buy me. What do I like? Give me walks on the beach with yummy morsels of sand under our feet. Lay me down on a trillion snowflakes as we make snow angels under the starry sky. Share with me deeply felt conversations.

### *My Beach Walk Home*

However, now, as my workday ends, I walk toward the water from the Castle, as the wind blows magical tunes into my ears while the waves crash up against my feet. Up ahead in front of the long, sandy pathway which leads me home to my Tiki sits a park bench waiting patiently for me. I am enough, and all that I am completes me. There's only room on that bench for me, Patricia Ann.

As I sit on the bench and think back on all those years of my generosity in giving my love, faithfulness, and commitment to others, I relax and drop deeper within realizing that no one needs anything from me, and no one wants anything from me. I am utterly calm in every fiber, nerve, and muscle in my body with my face basking in the direct sunlight. I relax and release healing light as my throat softens, breathing in a great sense of rest that nourishes the calm peace inside of me. My being is the most beautiful, timeless, and spaceless vessel of true paradise and heaven within.

I am so comfortable in my being as every part of me is relaxing so profoundly. In a place so soothing as though I'm in a dream, I fully embody all the complete and calm beauty of clarity inside me. I am receiving the love of pure peace in really trusting effortlessly in myself. As I meditate, settling gently inside my true, confident self, I can experience myself breathing comfortably and am watching from the outside in, observing and seeing myself filled with a sense of delight and joy in every part of my being. I am happy, settled and content in knowing who I am. I notice, as if in a movie, that I am still learning, watching myself filled with a sense of gratitude and ease, calm and objectivity, clear in the moment. I am worthy and deserving of my love, my strength, and my peace that I am learning in my way.

Life is coming back into me as I am becoming one with my highest expression and most confident self. I am discovering what I need as I am seeing myself exploring with a new level of clarity and self-compassion, becoming one with my happy self. I am experiencing this in each part of me, as though having always been led and controlled by my SPIRIT. My inner joy is allowing me to make my highest and wisest choices as I see things more clearly. My timeless SPIRIT is guiding my deepest learning in being present and loving myself. Being one as I breathe in healing throughout my mind, BODY, and CHILD.

### *My Vow*

I talked about how I discovered on Instant Media a post I had written about a vow I made five years ago about a silly golf game, but I expanded on it to claim my life and love as a commitment.

It's been exactly a year since I went through the Hoffman progress and had written a vow that stated a promise to myself, Patricia Ann, that my SPIRIT will lead me.

Here I sit, reflecting on my journey and how my true desires and dreams have and still are coming into fruition. All because I have written them down.

*My Fight Club Within* is written totally for me, by me as my commitment to how I fight my battles.

Transformation is solely up to you, and it doesn't matter if you're in confession, if you're in chapel, or if you're inside the prison walls of darkness, there is always a higher power that will give you answers and give you a way out. It all starts from within and reaching out to receive.

### *Sushi, Friendship, and Laughter*

I just enjoyed the best dinner ever at my favorite sushi restaurant with Liz, my second chapter beach yoga instructor. My first view of the Castle hosted Liz in the foreground, and she is my best friend that I've met here in Paradise. She also happens to be a contributing editor on *My Fight Club Within*.

Over dinner, as we were discussing the first nine chapters which she has read and is working on, I began to share the second part of the book which has a huge twist to it and how I was about to become serious with uncovering some deeply rooted facts.

However, that is all the further I could go as she was reflecting on one of the stories of me being in my little black dress in the scene in Ubud. Then she rolls into laughing so hard while I was trying to remember which account she's talking about. Of course, it was the one in Bali when I puked all inside my helmet in front of a glamorous five-star restaurant with people out front in their tuxedos and evening gowns. I burst with laughter, claiming how if that would have gotten on *YouTube*, I'd be rich.

She then tells me how drawn in and connected she feels while reading. It's like she's right there with me on the scene. This I would say is right up there as being one of the most embarrassing moments of my life. However, now it has turned out to be one of the most hilarious and fun moments – no matter what we are facing in any given moment, all we can do is be ourselves. Laughter is the best medicine that we can give and receive to ourselves and others.

### *My Learning Disability*

At the beginning of the next chapter, I write about my secret in having dyslexia. It's been so easy for me now to blurt it out and announce it to whom it may or may not concern. In the Castle, I teach ballroom dancing as an exercise program created by one of the famous instructors from *Dancing with the Stars*. How I learn is by watching and participating, not from studying on the computer or reading books. I must create my choreography and remember the different steps which consist of twelve ballroom moves – The Hustle/Disco, Foxtrot, Quickstep, Tango, Samba, Salsa, Cha-Cha, Paso Doble, Jive, Lindy Hop, Rumba, Merengue. Whew, that overwhelms me with just listing them here. Also, forget about me with typing, most of this book has been me using Siri, and then I copy and paste.

I thank God for having Liz as an editor and friend because she types it all up so quickly once I've got it all down. I've been hiding my secret of feeling stupid and different by working extra hard my whole life.

There are a few more humble others whose names aren't listed who have helped me tremendously, demonstrating their integrity by keeping the spotlight on my growth and success. They want me to glisten. This has been such a learning process for me in opening up with my vulnerability in receiving help with my dyslexia.

In teaching a class today, I had to apologize to a member for getting lost with my direction cues. "But I have Dyslexia", I announced to the whole class. Afterward I got several people who came up to me and said I am so good, one said I was the best instructor she's ever had. I felt so loved because I was able to receive praise after giving out my best.

However, just thinking about what I've written towards the end of this chapter takes my breath away. I'm hyperventilating and crying and trying to breathe all at the same time as I talk to Siri.

I'm back in the ring.

### *Grateful for My Tiki*

In my former life, when I was married and living in my million-dollar homes, my closet was bigger than the bedroom that I have now. It was full of things I hardly wore. Less is best for me now. I love wearing a uniform to the Castle and the Children's Hospital. All those other things I got rid of I don't miss one bit.

As I am getting closer and closer to the most challenging and most laborious chapter for me to reveal to you in Secrets, I am facing the biggest mountain head-on and plowing straight through with perseverance for me. My heart's desire is that my children will have a clearer understanding of me; the same that I now have after diligently unveiling my all.

I guess I began to fall apart like Humpty Dumpty when I moved here to Paradise. I waited and waited for all the king's horses and all the king's men to come and put me back together again.

Externally, I was doing stupid shit to my body and running far away from love and moved here to paradise.

I ran out of money and places on my body for more scars from doctors performing needless surgeries. Yes, I started being a cutter back in the early nineties with getting breast implants that I didn't need, I am a D cup, I then had them removed a few years later.

So, when I broke my toe, I went under the knife again, leaving significant scars on my upper and lower body. However, the two toe surgeries on the right big toe are the tiniest of scars compared to what I put my body through. I mean just stupid shit; I weigh one hundred and seventeen pounds and had no reason to have these superfluous surgeries. I even talked my best friend into taking care of me. I was relentless and would not allow her to talk me out of it. Of course, I didn't and could not tell my kids. Although they now know, and I know they think I'm a bit crazy for it.

I had to cause pain and see the results to be hurt and cut by the hands of a surgeon. I know it sounds insane, and I didn't understand why I was behaving like a crazy person back then, but it has become crystal clear to me now.

*This is how I fight my battles.*

## 11. Secrets

I have a learning disability. I am dyslexic. Until recently, this was a hidden secret that I kept to myself. My very intellectually strict dad took me to a psychiatrist at a very young age when I wasn't quite able to figure things out as quickly as he thought I should.

After a long week of enduring hours of testing each day in a room with this doctor in DC, he told me I was very creative and special, as he smiled. Then my dad shook his head and grabbed my hand, telling me, "Let's go home, Patsy."

I guess you can say I have spent a pretty large portion of my life trying to be normal like everyone else. It was so exhausting trying to be somebody that I am not.

One of the most loving, precious, and pivotal moments I experienced occurred with my beautiful daughter, Tatum, while hanging out on her sofa, I was in town and staying with her because I had all my things in storage while traveling the world with my Aussie boyfriend. For the first time, I was vulnerable, and I had opened up to her about my learning disability and how I felt stupid, unworthy, and not accomplished. As the tears poured out of me, she ever so gently held me tightly and said, "Mom, I so love and adore you. You are the most beautiful woman in the world to me. From my very start as a little girl you have always been my hero. All I ever wanted in life was to grow up and be just like you."

## *Dyslexia*

My friend, Darla, told me in March 2019 that she loves the changes in me that I now too am beginning to see through my all-consuming new world of writing.

Last eight months, I have isolated myself deep in work, allowing for a nightly heartfelt conversation of our day.

This is the most radical but surreal move for me when I decided to be a writer; learning what I need in merely being me. This is me in going about my business of figuring out who I am and what I want on a daily day to day, moment to moment basis. Yes, I am a full-time serious writer, and yes, I am unique in how I work.

My life has changed drastically since coming out of the closet with my dyslexia. I am now self-publishing my very first book, *My Fight Club Within*. Since the age of ten, I've kept my secret buried and covered deeply inside me, acting out daily trying desperately to be normal like everybody else. I realize now that what I once thought was embarrassing, has turned out to be the most beautiful gift that I treasure in myself, and now I give freely to the world.

How did I accomplish this impossible mission when words are, but a scrambled mess, and I see only pictures in my brain? My hard work consisted of my journeys transformed verbally from my head by Siri onto iPhone into notes, then copied and pasted into the creation of MFCW.

Step 1. Awareness – if I feel (The moment I became aware.)

Step 2. Action – I can heal (Came out from within.)

Step 3. Allow – and be real (I embraced all of myself and at the same time, becoming aware of how my Dyslexia was indeed a big plus, a superpower that I now walk freely in.)

## *Learning to Accept Me*

With having dyslexia but hiding it in the closet, my most challenging job was sitting behind a desk full time for a university in the administration Records Department. I would help advise students to register and enroll in choosing their classes for Fall/Winter semester. This was the only type of job I could have for the year 2016 because of my broken toe.

The combination of sitting for eight solid hours in front of a computer, while looking up college majors was the deadliest for me. I would run out the door and drive to the nearest park on my hour lunch break. There I would lie on my back next to the fountain and look up at the sky for forty-five minutes. I can't stand being closed in an office while sitting still. It was brutal as I was the only one standing and doing squats behind my desk while talking on the phone to students begging me for favors that I couldn't give.

That last job was harder on me than the breakup from my boyfriend; I kid you not.

Having dyslexia and writing a book is the hardest thing I've ever done in my entire life as this book covers many subject matters that are seldom discussed out loud, let alone to be written about.

Some subject matters have caused me horrific pain in going back in time. However, I had to go back to face up and feel acceptance so I could find out what I honestly do want. Honestly, I am so far out of my comfort zone, but at the same time have never felt more surreal in translating my pictures into words in *My Fight Club Within*. I pray my work here depicts my brain and its gift of quirkiness to you.

Now that I have come out with my secret of having dyslexia, I can't begin to explain if it was more work in hiding it; then surviving it? All the energy and time I've spent going against my real self to fit in with other people. All that time of just thinking, *Oh, if only I could be more like my super amazingly intelligent ex-husband, lover, or friend.*

Don't even mention my many hours of entertainment in displaying my charm of witty mass-producing efforts to make me more like you. Oh, how exhausting it was to be always disappointed in myself and others. Those days are now becoming further and further behind me as I have said NO MORE to those past mistakes, disappointments, and people that have let me down over and over and over again because I have stopped letting myself down and gotten off that roller coaster. I have finally learned how to say "No" to other people and pleasing them with what they want and "Yes" now to me in knowing just exactly what I want and need. So, this is the beautiful question I ask myself every single day, "What do I want?"

I guess what Darla means in seeing a significant change in me is that I stand up for myself now. Sure, it may have been a lot safer and easier as I hid behind my mask, but now that I've come out and I'm me; I am no longer on the sidelines as the spectator. I am now the main character as being myself in my movie, and I'm kicking ass in spelling out my picture world of words for you.

Being myself is the coolest, most fabulous, and wonderful ride to be on. Nowadays, when people compliment me, I believe them full heartily as I am aware of embracing and showing off my superpowers – my season, my timing. Returning to my mantra from the Introduction:

Step 1. Awareness – if I feel

Step 2. Action – I can heal

Step 3. Allow – and be real

Awareness took place in that moment of expressing and revealing my true inner feelings.

Action arose in boldly speaking the truth in that moment, and the healing began to take root.

Allowing me to be truly my authentic self.

*This is how I fight my battles.*

## Secrets - Part Two

I'm about to disclose the biggest secret I've ever kept; a secret I've never shared with any other human being, not a soul.

Maybe that's the reason and my soul purpose for writing this book.

In fact, I was about to finish my book without this Part Two, when my business advisor, Jim, asked me an important question. What is the outcome you desire through publishing this book?

My immediate answer was to generate an income. He then recommended that I needed to expand each chapter. I have been torn up inside debating on if I should or even if I could divulge my secret, especially with how this will dramatically affect my kids.

It is the most critical decision, and I feel it needs to be out in the open, and my adult children I know will suffer.

However, they deserve to know the truth, and that is what I have tried to demonstrate as their mother throughout their entire life; that the truth will set you free.

## *More Dark Uglies*

However, before I reveal, I find it imperative that I share some more of my dark uglies. They are not secrets, as my family knows about them. But you, the reader, must know too.

I have always felt that I have grown by leaps and bounds with forgiveness towards my parents, past relationships, and all others who have hurt me. However, do you know what? I may call them dark uglies, but they have become the beautiful scars that I've made and carried deep within me.

At this moment, my tummy is beginning to feel heavy, and I'm getting that knot in my throat. I am now going to acknowledge and notice them, feel them, and allow myself to explain to you why the throat. You see, my dad was so strict and protective over me that he kept track of my every move, knowing my whereabouts at all times. If I was to attend a Catholic Youth Organization (CYO) dance, he would take me and chaperone. There would be no dancing or me talking to another boy; not on his watch.

I was eleven years old, and a boy got a hold of my phone number and called me. My dad answered the call, wrote down all his information before hanging up the phone receiver. He then grabbed me by my neck and hung me up on the wall threatening me while choking me at the same time. He yelled that he would kill me before I become a tramp and a whore like my mother. I begged and pleaded for my life, "No, Daddy, please, please! I promise I will never be like her."

## *Changing Schools*

When I was sixteen years old, I ran away from my dad to live with my mom. What a culture shock for me. From an all-girls Catholic high school to public school.

The Catholic school had been difficult. My dad wanted me to go, but after my first few days there, all I did was complain to my dad about the algebra and how much I hated it, and I didn't understand one thing about it.

As I was leaving, my dad came out of the school, waving some papers and said, "Listen to me, Patsy. Here is your test paper with the highest score of the class A plus, so please, explain to me how you don't understand algebra?"

I have no idea how I got an A, and I felt zero confidence walking into my first day of public school. It was chaos with the desks all turned around and in disarray, and the kids sitting with their feet propped upon them. Guys and girls wore jeans, chewed gum, and talked out loud at the same time with absolutely no regard or acknowledgment of the teacher in the front of the room.

I had come from complete structure where every desk was in a line facing the front. All of us students were dressed alike as we wore the same uniform. Girls wore a plaid jumper over a crisp, white, starched blouse and navy-blue knee-high socks with black and white Oxford Saddle shoes. Boys wore navy blue trousers with suit jackets to match along with white starched shirts with blue ties and wingtip shoes on their feet.

As soon as our teacher, a priest, mother superior, or nun would enter the classroom, we, the girls, would curtsy, and the boys would bow with a greeting of "Good morning", or "Good afternoon, sister".

### *My First Love*

When I was seventeen, I was a junior in high school having the reputation of being one of the only virgins at that age. Until one sunny afternoon, my best friend asked me to walk over to her cousin's house, where we cut through the woods from school.

On that very walk, I laid my eyes on Brian. It was love at first sight. My first words to her were, "I'm in love."

Brian graduated, and my mother issued the ultimatum of either me quitting school and getting a job to help her out or moving back in with my dad. So, I went to work to help my mom.

## *Working Girl*

I did some modeling jobs from the age of sixteen. Once at an Air Show, I went up in a hot-air balloon with the Fifth Dimension as they performed the famous song, *Up, Up and Away*.

I also modeled and was centerfold for a *Pilots Preflight Magazine* as Miss November, standing barefoot on a pumpkin wearing a pilgrim outfit. Then one page for a close-up in a sexy V-neck sweater with my face near the body of the plane.

Brian went far away and out to sea, joining the navy, and I went through six excruciating weeks of Bunny School. I became the youngest Playboy Bunny at the time, making more money than I knew how to spend.

## *Bunny School*

Going through Bunny School, I learned an entirely new set of skills, such as how to walk with books on my head. I went from doing the curtsy for the nuns to doing the bunny dip with my cottontail pointing toward the food and drinks for businessmen and famous athletes.

That's when I discovered that I had a real talent for making and closing sales. For example, I was the customer service bunny wearing a sash across my fitted, patented gold suit. There would maybe be just one member with eleven guests around the big round table having lunch. They thought I was the Bunny of the Year and called me over to join them. I would sit with my legs crossed, signing up all the eleven guests for possible membership at twenty-five dollars a person for my commission.

I also played bumper pool, a dollar per game, win or lose. Small bets under the table would add up because I could never lose.

Even though my dad didn't talk to me, I still felt good about myself and having this awesome job and making so much money. Yes, there were some activities and shady stuff going on inside the Club with the older girls, but I didn't participate in it. I was the baby there, and I was special and spoiled. I even kept my morals when I was offered to do the centerfold for $10,000. I said no. I also got offered $5,000 to pose in *Penthouse*. Even though my mom begged me to do it, because she wanted me to make money, I was keeping my promise to my dad.

I would mainly work as door bunny, greeting the guests when they arrived. Also, I would work as a giftshop bunny, where I would eat ice cream and read some of the articles in the *Playboy* magazine that I sold behind the counter.

A member once offered me fifty dollars for my cottontail, which was simply a small clip-on piece kept in the dressing room in a large container. It snapped onto my patented special made suit that fit my body perfectly. I felt like a movie star when being in the dressing room and having my own seamstress and hairdresser making me beautiful. Of course, I always had my morals and told the guy he could purchase a tail on a beautiful wooden plaque. I would never break the law by allowing any part of my patented suit to leave the Club.

Still being a teenager, the legal age to enter the club was twenty-one, and so all my guy friends were never able to come and see me in my uniform. Although I was once featured on the cover of the VIP magazine as door bunny, my mom lost or threw away all the magazines that I was featured.

PATRICIA SIMON

## *Playboy Magazine Article Saves My Life*

In one of the *Playboy* articles that I read while at work, it talked about how to prevent being raped. The article said that if you lock your legs by twisting your feet tightly together, then that would make it difficult for a man to put his penis in you.

It was maybe a few nights later when I was out with all my friends. Yes, they were mostly guys because girls hated me thinking I would steal their boyfriends. I have never done that, by the way. However, guys loved and respected me because I had class and values. So, one of the guys that I didn't know that well said, "Hey, Patty, let me give you a ride home. I have some good weed that I want to stop and pick up for my girlfriend at a motel room."

We made the stop, and I went in with him, but then he immediately grabbed me and ripped my shirt. He threw me up against the wall and window, breaking some blinds off. He threw me down on the bed and covered up my mouth to stop my screams as he proceeded to try to enter my body. My legs were so tightly locked he could not enter. Then I gasped for breath pretending I could not breathe. He got worried, I guess, thinking he was killing me. I fought and threw him off me and ran out for my life.

I went home and didn't leave the house for three weeks. I immediately told all my guy friends. Many girls came forward and said he had raped them. My neighborhood guy friends went after him, and he may still be in a wheelchair to this day. I don't know or even want to know, but I am grateful to have read that article that helped me fight off my rapist.

The Playboy Club would soon close. My first love, Brian, was far, far away, and I got pregnant by a wealthy guy. This guy was the one who hooked me up with my job as a bunny. He also convinced me to abort our baby. He could be very persuasive, and I did what I was told. I had just turned eighteen. Those were the darkest and heaviest moments, as I descended into the most profound sorrow of my most considerable loss.

## *My Baby*

My baby. The greatest, most significant part of me that I destroyed. That day would become the start of my body's self-destruction.

I would go to perform this deadly act by myself while my driver waited for me outside in the parking lot of the clinic. I went inside with three hundred dollars cash in my hand and handed it over at the front desk. I was taken back to a small room where I lay back on a gurney and cried and cried and cried.

I think I was awake during the procedure, and after the murder, I insisted that I see my baby that was being taken out of me.

The doctor and nurse frantically proceeded to try to talk me out of it, telling me that it would be a sight for my eyes to see.

I was adamant in not taking no for an answer. I wanted to see exactly what I've done to my baby.

The doctor went over grabbing a large glass jar from a shelf nearby that was full of cut-up parts and pieces of my baby.

From that moment on, I made a promise to myself that I would never share or speak of this day of what I had done. I erased my baby and the man who impregnated me permanently as if he never existed.

Even until this very day, I've never let go; in my heart, I am forever linked tightly to my baby. We are still connected just as I am with my great-great-grandmother, whom I met in the first six months of my own life. The beautiful woman, my grandmother, who I never met, gave birth to my mom, and died when my mom was just two years old. We are linked and connected. I know in my heart and hold on to knowing that our SPIRITS of oneness will be timelessly bonded and spend together many moons of that time in a heaven that is within my reach.

This day as it is written here on these pages, my baby will be recognized, seen, heard and signified as one of my greatest accomplishments, most importantly, being a part of my being as are all of my children, Tatum, Patrick, and John, my children that I have loved and wanted from the beginning in my womb.

## *Having Sex on the First Date*

It was shortly after, a matter of a couple of months, that I met my first husband, the only man that I ever brought home to my dad's house. My father and brother both tried to beat him up in the driveway because they didn't think we should date. So no, I wasn't pregnant, but a month later we had a huge wedding in the big Catholic Church that my grandfather founded and built. I didn't want to marry him. The only reason I did was that we had sex. I was still in mourning of losing my baby. I was deeply, deeply depressed. I didn't even want to be alive.

Still, only eighteen years young, I attempted to end my life by taking all my mother's prescription downers from her medicine cabinet.

## *Near-Death Experience*

I succeeded. My mother had called the hospital while having me propped up on pillows. They told her it was too late for me. I only remember being on the outside of me, high up near the ceiling, looking down at my mom and hearing her desperate cries. She held my hand and pleaded, "Patsy, please, please don't die! I love you."

I then felt as if I were magnetically drawn upward toward an endless tunnel of the most powerful circle of pure light. It was brighter than the sun. I was overwhelmed and felt nothing but pure love in wanting to go up and through the tunnel.

However, then I heard my mother's cry, "Patsy, please don't die. Stay with me!"

I felt my body jerk up, and my arms flew upward as well. I came back to my mom.

It took me months to recover, and I was so weak.

My NDE, (near-death experience) is not a secret. However, there is no doubt in me that I know that I know that I know that there is a place called eternity where our spirit dwells and lives on. I know that's where my baby is, and I will do whatever it takes in the universe to live in love for connection with my child.

I now knew I had a purpose.

Brian had come home from the Navy to find me married.

I was settling into my marriage after getting our place. My husband was doing well with his career. I was learning how to cook and decorate our new place. Then out of the clear blue, I get a phone call of devastating news that Brian was dead at the age of twenty-one. He'd died of a drug overdose. I lost it.

### *Brian is Dead*

I left my husband and went to the funeral to be with Brian's family, driving in the limo with his casket. My only copy of the *Pilots Preflight Magazine* where I was Miss November, was placed under his head. I couldn't stop kissing his cold purple lips. I still loved him.

My deepest kept secret is now no more a secret. Yes, I am fully acknowledging my many years of isolation and shame that I hid from the entire world, even though I am experiencing the darkest and deepest gut-wrenching sorrow in doing so. It was sacred to me. My greatest love. My baby.

And, my first love, Brian, who was gone.

All that I desired and prayed for in my marriage was to have my baby girl Tatum.

And now all my brokenness and the pieces that were buried and deeply hidden are all coming to light by my SPIRIT within. I have let go. I have released and relinquished all my secrets.

*This is how I fight my battles.*

## 12. Death

Today, January 25, 2019, is exactly four years since I watched my mother's spirit leave her body. I had said my goodbyes via FaceTime on a Tuesday as they had taken her off life support, removing all food and water. The following Sunday, my daughter phoned and said, "Mom, she's waiting for you." I immediately boarded a plane, and I was off to a small town in South Carolina. I arrived by noon.

She was lying there staring off, the death rattle escaping her tiny throat, as I sat with her singing and encouraging her to let go. Only five months earlier, while visiting her in the nursing home she was begging me to kill her; she was suffering and in so much pain, and I felt it.

The first time I went to visit was in the fall around Halloween. I went out and bought her several little outfits, a Star Magazine, and her favorite candy corn. I decorated her room, and the nurses all raved about how fun she was with making her bed and helping in the kitchen. Next thing you know, my mom is choking on the candy corn. I ran to get the nurse, and they began doing CPR. I guess I really could have fulfilled her wish at that time in killing her.

She was so adorable later that week, sitting in the hall near the nursing station eating her little half sandwich and her favorite UTZ potato chips that I had bought her. I then passed the chips around to the other older, lonely people.

I had been in hiding from my stalker at the time, so I had a rental car. I drove it from my cousin's house to see my mom for a few days staying in a hotel nearby. She was so excited to see me, and it was heart-wrenching when I prepared to leave as she too was ready with her sweater on as if to go home with me.

The older people wore alarms on their ankles, so it was immediately known if they were to roam past the safe areas. Security was tight, and the doors had to be locked. It was awful hearing that buzzer going off. I thought there'd be no way I could ever stay in a place like that. However, I almost had to as when leaving; I was putting something into my trunk and accidentally locked my keys inside. It was around 11:00 p.m. when the locksmith arrived.

### *My Mother's Beautiful Love*

Even though there was a long distance between us, we spoke every day on the phone. It was like Groundhog Day with the same conversation of "Hello, honey, how are you?"

"I'm good, Mom. You?"

"I'm okay. Have you met anybody yet?"

I would typically reply no, until one day I lied, "Yes, Mom, I have, and I'm engaged, so there is no more need to hang on. You can let go, Mom."

On one day, our conversation was different.

It went like this. "Hi, honey."

"Hi, Mom, how are you?"

"I'm good, honey, and you?"

"I'm okay, Mom."

My mom then replied, "I love you so much honey, and soon, as I go up in the sky, I'm going to be loving you all the way up, telling you how much I love you." "Thank you, Mom. I love you so much too."

So, when I met her doctor, we immediately bonded in a great conversation about my mom's wishes. She said I would be amazed at how many adult kids are happy to keep their parents alive suffering, just for the mere fact that they are still alive.

I said, "Oh, no, please if you can, up her morphine."

She agreed but felt I would probably be there through the night because my mom has a strong heart.

By now it was 4:20 p.m. and I wandered off to find the cafeteria, which I found closed. The small-town hospital felt very empty as I roamed down the corridors and back to peek into the room. I didn't see any changes in my mom.

### *Two Angels*

Then, much to my surprise, I saw two beautiful, exotic, darkhaired women wearing white coats coming toward me saying, "Come now; it's your mom's time."

I looked up and said, "Really?" as the three of us walked into the room.

They stood on each side of her bed as I leaned over her. One woman said, "Look, she's reaching up for you."

My mom reached up with her hands and grabbed me by the back of my head, looking into my eyes, and in a shallow, hollow voice, she said, "I love you."

The women at that moment were embracing each other with laughter and chuckles of joy. As I stood over watching my eighty-four-year-old mom transforming into a youthful radiant woman, with her beautiful eyes gazing back to me, what was even more astonishing was that she was not breathing. I asked, "How could this be? She is so alive with expressing her face and trying to talk but has no breath."

"Yes, but her heart is still beating." Then, they said, "She's gone."

I looked up at the clock, and it said 5:00 p.m. so, I asked, "What is her time of death?"

They said, "Somebody will be here to tell you," and then they vanished.

I don't know if they were angels, but I do believe they were my mom's.

*Hebrews 13:2 (King James Version) – "Be not forgetful to entertain strangers: for thereby some have entertained angels unawares."*

### We Talked Every Day

Practically every day for the past ten years or more, my mother would call me, or I would call her, and we would talk; especially in her last three years, we never missed a day.

That was probably one of the darkest periods of my life – going through a divorce and being on my own for the first time since being a teenager. My mom never left my side or my corner, consistently showing and giving me all her love and support. It wasn't always like that, at least not in the beginning.

## *Forgiveness*

I was the youngest, and my mom didn't want another baby. In fact, she abandoned me when I was five years old. She left my dad and went off and lived with a man who was abusive to her.

She was proven unfit, and the courts gave my dad full custody of me. My greatest childhood memories of happiness, joy, and fulfillment were spending time with my mother on Sundays and holidays.

Did I go through a period in my life where I was angry and bitter at my mom? Yes, it was by far one of the greatest and hardest struggles of my life; my thorn – forgiving her. So, does that make me unique for being her only focus in her last days, knowing only me, as I was, her only adult daughter? Absolutely!

I fell asleep watching Ruth last night on Netflix, right after the part where her dad had sold her to the Moabites. Watching her beginning felt a lot like mine. However, what a beautiful ending to her life's journey!

I realize now that my mom was with me too, on my deathbed, back when I was a teenager.

I feel from that day a part of me remained dead, as I so wanted to enter the tunnel of light. I have always had one fingertip or two still within reach.

## *My Dad's Beautiful Workmanship*

After the death of my dad in 2005, Iris and I met at the airport to take care of my dad's funeral and then prepare his house for sale.

We worked so hard cleaning and ripping up carpet to unmask the beautiful, solid-wood floors. We had a huge yard sale and stayed upstairs in our usual bedrooms, falling asleep exhausted each night.

The change was so remarkable in how beautiful my dad's home was after a much-needed woman's touch.

We made all three floors into a showcase of the years of my dad's woodworking and engineering talents. This house was built solid like the Castle in which I worked. It was a fortress, with cherry wood adorning the walls and the cabinetry in the kitchen, down in the basement. When I was a child, I would play hours of shuffleboard by a large dance floor that was mostly taken up with the two sawhorses that were holding up whatever my dad was working on at the time. I would usually be with him, on one end, holding the wood steady as he cut.

Most of my childhood was spent assisting my dad in tearing down and rebuilding our home. I understand now why I had such a joy in moving around with my husband and family and building six houses together, each different and unique. I would design and work closely with each of the builders in creating our dream homes. My husband trusted me and my abilities to create the perfect atmosphere, giving me full rein. There was nothing more satisfying than to see the bones of the home where our family would dwell come to life.

### *Dad's Ghost*

Iris and I were relishing in the results of all our hard labor as we were both upstairs getting cleaned up to celebrate with a dinner out, finally. We then heard a noise downstairs coming from the living room. As we ran down the steps, we noticed that the lamp that was always turned on was knocked off the end table.

We freaked out and knew there was no coincidence or randomness to this happening. My dad always had a light on; the lamp on the table.

He always made sure and had the porch light on for me and even installed an automatic light that would appear the moment my tractor key would touch the alarm system.

So, when that lady in the Castle where I work asked me if I believe in ghosts, easily, I reply, "Yes, indeed, I do."

The Holy Ghost is the same as the divine SPIRIT of God that I feel is connected as one in my SPIRIT.

### *Another Close Call with a Near-Death Experience (NDE)*

Life is so much more than what we're seeing. If the sky begins to fall on me, know I am forgiven. I know I'm walking in love, the source of my strength that arises from within.

In Mexico, in 2018, I came close to another NDE as I came down with the highest of fevers. I became so dehydrated and weak that my Aussie boyfriend carried me into the small-town hospital. They kept me hooked up to IV fluids and under constant watch. My boyfriend never left my side.

I lost so much fluid, drenching the bed until it was soaking wet. I was delirious with my fever as my boyfriend reported overhearing me softly singing hymns of scripture that I guess I must have memorized somewhere along the way. I don't remember much myself, except how lovely my boyfriend was in being so attentive; he spent the time trying to feed me and make me drink water, which I hadn't the strength in me to do.

The next day, he once again carried my soaking wet, weak body, wrapped in a blanket, back into the hospital. They again hooked me up to the IV and worked to break the fever when suddenly the blood test results came back, concluding that I had a bad case of salmonella. I had never been so cared for except by my parents and great grandmother; I knew my boyfriend loved me.

## *I Love Nature, But I Love People More*

Disappointment at the beginning of my move here was lurking around me in every corner. As my teacher, Raz, brought to my attention, my conversations were full of life events resulting in my disappointment in people, but I always lit up when it came to being immersed in nature.

Was I blinded by the light? Certainly not mine. I feel I was mainly disappointed with myself for allowing other people's fucked-up stories of their disappointments in themselves to wedge in between my path.

I was struggling until my good friend, Darla, stepped in, consistently available to hold me accountable in keeping to my vows to love myself. After all, she has a big stake in the outcome of this book, as she wants her healthy, happy, and positive best friend back.

So now, when I run into people with my attitude of disappointment, Darla reminds me, as she eloquently states, "Pat, think about it. Their actions have not changed, they are still the same, but you have, and they can't control you any longer."

I no longer allow and give my time and energy by subjecting my SPIRIT to the old dead me. A lot has to do with my disconnecting from the torment of guilt and replacing it with forgiveness to receive the love that I have been so deserving of within myself.

I guess this chapter on death is more about life for me because it was the turning point where I had to die totally to myself, sorrow, and pain. Beginning from the end, back to the start and around halfway, to be present now in this moment.

### *Before This is What I Thought I Wanted to Be*

I wanted to be Miss Goody Two-Shoes and desired to be the best at everything I do. I wanted to be the best wife, the best mother, the best nana, the best friend, the best cook, the best lover, the best girlfriend, the best dancer, etc., etc., etc.; especially after losing my mother, I started to bury myself even further down with all my secrets of pain and sorrow. My secrets, dyslexia, abortion, and others felt suffocating.

I have been busy performing my many talents as I started dancing on my toes at six months old. By the age of four, my grandfather would pay me to watch me dance to "Yakety Sax". I just had to Google it because, of course, I don't remember. All I can do is picture me dancing my moves away.

I can't stop, and frankly, I won't quit at performing and giving my best in all I do. However, I now give my best to me first.

There is nothing sexier than my authentic self.

So just as I end *My Fight Club Within* on Change, Chapter 17, it was also my original subject matter when outlining the book back in January 2017. *My Fight Club Within* began in October 2018 with me starting entirely over in being homeless, jobless, and alone.

I liken my book to a puzzle with many broken pieces from my past and present life stories that I am slowly connecting, designing my placement of me, Patricia Ann. My soul awakens with you and how we are all on these pages connected into a place for our healing. Maybe your soul desires a will for change to begin for you, to awaken and assemble your pieces in building your beautiful new life.

I've changed! It's never, never too late. You can too!

*This is how I fight my battles.*

## 13. Spiritual Warfare

On the front cover of *My Fight Club Within* is a photograph that was taken many years ago of a sunset somewhere in the Midwest. I don't know who took it or even how it got into my hands. However, it has become one of my most prized possessions that hangs up high on my wall.

On the right half of the picture, I see an Angel. After displaying the photo for over ten years hanging on my wall, my son Patrick came into my room one day, and said, "Mom, that's a creepy and ugly demon staring into the face of the angel."

"What! Where?" I said. "I don't see it!"

It was at that very moment when I finally saw it. There it was just as clear as day – it's pointy ears and beady eyes staring up at my beautiful angel. Patrick and I immediately in unison uttered, "Wow, this is spiritual warfare."

Oh, how freaky and weird that was for me. Talk about the heebie-jeebies! I took the picture down and put it in the closet and tried to forget about it. To have something before your eyes and not see the obvious. After all, my thoughts were "Hell no" in my Alabama accent at the time as this east coast girl was trying to fit in as a southern belle in my showcase home. No way will I have that ugly demon with my beautiful angel displayed on my wall. I was torn.

This is my shortest chapter because there is no better way to explain it then by sight of my book cover of *My Fight Club Within*; for you to see it directly through the eyes of the beholder.

*This is how I fight my battles.*

## 14. Soul Awakening

It was soon after the discovery of the demon in my Spiritual Warfare picture, towards the end of January 2009, and I was still married, and my husband was working out of town; all my kids were away at school. I was alone in the big empty house with my four-legged best friend, Cookie. At 5:00 a.m., I awoke to an astounding voice that echoed out, "Patricia Ann, it is time for you to wake up now. Patricia Ann, it is time for you to wake up now."

I was shaken and chilled to my bones as I arose and leaped out of bed, shouting out, "Who are you? Who is there?"

I immediately grabbed the phone and the alarm clock asking again, "Who is this, who is here? Please, please answer!" No response. There was no one there.

Later that day, my son, Patrick, had come home, and I shared with him what had happened. I was still shaken to my very core by that voice, like no other, and how it repeated twice and called out my name. It was clearly the most brilliant, masculine yet feminine, and perfect tone of authority, an alive sounding vibration to my ears that immediately woke me from a deep morning sleep.

Patrick then shared with me a CD by Jason Upton that he wanted me to hear. I listened while he played it on the computer. He asked that I pay close attention and listen to hear if that was like what I had heard earlier in that same likeness of voice. I listened; goosebumps rose and took hold of my entire body as I listened in awe. "Yes, Oh my God!"

Then he shared the story of Jason Upton, a soloist who was performing somewhere in the Midwest before a live audience. Shortly after his performance, a twelve-year-old boy came up to the artist and said how he enjoyed his band.

Jason said, "There is no band. It was just me by myself." The boy proceeded to say, "Oh no, there was you and all your choir, dressed in white singing in the background with you." Please, go ahead, *Google* it.

### *My Wake-up Call*

Since that very day, I believe, wholeheartedly, that it was God who woke me up and told me, "Patricia Ann, it is time for you to wake up now. Patricia Ann, it is time for you to wake up now."

So, I began to face my demons by proudly displaying once again one of my most prized possessions of art. Not only back up on my wall, but now I want to share it with the entire world; my photo of the demon and the angel that is now on the front cover of this book. Now you have the full story of my picture of Spiritual Warfare captured up in the sky for you and me.

Be aware that you may not see the angel and demon at first. In fact, there are some friends that still have not been able to see. Please be kind and patient with yourself and don't allow my beliefs, your beliefs, or un-beliefs to have space for room of any judgment.

## *MFCW Book Cover Description*

My best way to describe this picture for you is that the angel takes up the entire middle and right side all in white and rose and outlined in light gold. The height and width of the angel take up far more space than the demon, starting at the very top of the pure white wing. It's majestically large, with deep tones of gold color crown on top of its head, which is in front of the white wing. Under the crown, tumbles thick, curly, golden hair, outlining the side profile of the face and around the left ear. The angel's detailed side profile is directly gazing over its own white rounded shoulder blade with the wing adjacent upward toward the top. You can see an all-white face from the side, with the forehead deeply darker in gold tone, drawing down to the humble dark golden left brow with the perfect white nose, lips, and chin outlined lightly. You'll see just a small, almost circular shape of black sky in between the chin, wing, and round shoulder and only the top part of the white neck and chest. Remember that all the angel is white with gold lining throughout. Surrounding the angel on the very top center and top right you'll notice rays of lavender and rose, unlike the familiar color scale. The picture has many orbs of different shades of rose, white, gold, and pink.

The demon is much smaller with its bald, coned head on the very left side of the picture. It appears to be looking out into the black sky not even seeing the angel dominating over it. There is only a tad bit of a dot of white on the right side of the demon's big, ugly, deformed nose with no brightness or shadows of light. The entire demon is a mere smudge of a smeared dark reddish black on the lower left-hand side of the picture. What I noticed most prominently when I became aware of the creature is its pointed ears and specks for its beady black eyes.

I feel there is never a time that I must wait for my angel to appear for my angel is with me at all times. I am convinced wholeheartedly that on January 25, 2015, when my mom died, not only just my angel but also my mom's angel was there together in connection in love for us.

Angels are omni.

*This is how I fight my battles.*

### It's Heaven for Me

For me, I choose Heaven. I choose Heaven, now here, on earth. My direction comes from the light of my SPIRIT, and I choose love, which is always present and within my reach, as my passage through the portal.

We all agree and believe that we will die, but we are not able to predict or know the exact hour. As far as thinking where our spirit goes from death is where we all differ. Some believe in Heaven and Hell. Some believe we reincarnate coming back again as another person, animal, or thing, and some believe we go back into the soil/ground within our dead bones.

After continuously searching for that perfect rhyme of light that I experienced in my NDE (near-death experience) way back when I was a teenager… I finally get it! The tunnel entrance was within my arm's reach as my body jerked upward into the light. That same scene would play out as I watch my mother's arms reach up at me as her spirit was leaving her body in her last moments of life.

Could I have had that most beautiful and amazingly loving connection with my mom if I was full of anger and unforgiveness? I think not.

### *Alzheimer's*

Doctors could not explain why it was only me my mom could recognize as she battled the deadly disease of Alzheimer's. Her brain was being eaten away with holes by the deadly disease, forgetting everybody. However, she remembered me. Her heart was beating in wait of me; her SPIRIT kept her alive without food and water for five days waiting for connection with me. That could've never been done without pure, unconditional love.

Heaven was within her reach.

So maybe that makes sense as far as me never being disappointed with nature in my atmosphere.

I had only clearly seen just the light (angel) with my eyes in the picture while the demon's beady eyes were there in the dark all along.

My angel is and was here all along, guarding my soul against the demon that wants total control of me.

I know without a doubt that the sole purpose of me being here in this universe is to love. This helps me to stay faithfully connected in being transparent in writing *My Fight Club Within*. So, when that hour comes when I take my last breath, I will be uplifted in Heaven with all my loved ones.

## Soul Awakening - Part Two

I was nine years old, and my dad was a member of PWP (Parents Without Partners). He was dating and had a lady friend come over to our house with her three-year-old little boy. I was out in the front yard playing ball with him, and my dad told me not to go out of the yard. My ball rolled over into the next-door neighbor's driveway that was adjacent to our front lawn. I quickly ran over and got the ball back from the neighbor's yard. At the same time my dad came out and called me into the house. He took me into the bathroom and proceeded to pull my ponytail while holding his hand tightly over my mouth to cover my cry.

He smacked my head so hard into the tile wall that I saw stars.

Okay, again, I am sharing with you the most terrifying, horrific, and downright despicable acts of abuse on a helpless little girl. However, that is now only a memory of a bitter experience from a sick and angry man, my dad, who over and over again begged me to forgive him. I would, and I did, and I still do. However, what if he hadn't? What value would my sharing these most painful memories have to serve for you and me?

## *My Dad's Love and Forgiveness*

I have shared much of his goodness with you, that of which I choose to remember in keeping deeply in my heart. He never let me go to sleep without hugging me and telling me that he loved me, which brings me back to that very same bathroom later that same painful day. I was taking a bath, and I had my first visit with my angel. Yes, she appeared out of nowhere and looked to be around eighteen years old with long brown hair. She played and covered me in endless bubbles that seem to last forever. It was pure bliss with much joy of laughter and splashes between us.

I remember much laughter and bubbles and the long string of soap hanging gracefully with the angel making images with bubbles all over my face. It was one of the most beautiful experiences I've ever had. The second was my mother's death. I was not frightened at all and yes, she did say let's play, and it was just joyful and as if time stood still.

## *Three B's – Busy, Being, and Baths*

Being a Regional Vice President in 1995, working full-time out of my home, running a successful business, being a supportive wife, and busy mother to my three kids, I was always busy being, but never too busy for my bubble baths.

My neighbor had told me a sad story about a pregnant sixteen-year-old in the hospital about to give birth to twins. She gave birth to two healthy and beautiful baby boys. That was a miracle because the father was not only a drug addict but a dealer as well.

They lived in a bad section of town where one day I had the sheriff, my neighbor, meet me at their apartment. I pretended and introduced him as my cousin. I would take them food and clothes that I would purchase for the twins at the Baby Gap.

I was working closely with her dad and knew she was about to lose her babies to him in a custody battle.

Her mother had died from cancer when she was five years old. Her dad remarried soon after. One day the stepmother was giving this sweet little five-year-old a bath. The preschooler was crying, missing her mom. The stepmom told her to stop her crying because her mom is dead, and she's not coming back.

I found out that the mother who had passed had three sisters, and one was a doctor who lived in Hawaii. The dad gave me power of attorney to help his daughter to travel to Hawaii so she could get away from the drug dealer boyfriend and start a new life with her aunt and babies. I was filled with joy as I got ahold of the girl (let's call her Ashley) and brought her into my home.

Immediately I filled my Jacuzzi tub full of bubbles. As I led her over to the side of the tub, I noticed the biggest and most horrendous scar covering her belly. I gently washed her body while listening to her tell me how wonderfully awesome she felt, and yes, she agreed to go to paradise with me. I then dressed her in a sweet dress of mine and even gave her my favorite sandals as we wore the same size.

The next day I was devastated, as Ashely had decided against Hawaii, and in doing so, gave up her babies. The dad and stepmother got custody of the twins, and she stayed with the boyfriend who is now in prison.

Today, Ashley is married and has her children together playing the piano beautifully, just as her mother played.

There are happy endings when love comes first.

I know I had some short conversations when I needed to apologize to my children, especially to my youngest son, who is a very competitive, athletic, and an incredibly brilliant man. I had to miss a few of his games and band practices as he received the honored first chair designation.

However, I know today, my kids know for sure and understand that when their mom was MIA that there was a good reason. I still only take baths, never a shower, unless there is no tub.

## *My Dream of Heaven*

Back when my kids were all at home, I had gotten sick one late night in 2000. I had collapsed onto the floor in the bathroom. My husband wasn't very warm towards my breakdown and was more upset that I woke him up and soon went right back to sleep.

It was in those moments that I tried to compose myself by quietly tiptoeing back all the way around to my side of the bed to not disturb him. I prayed silently, and I asked God to please take me away from this. And, He answered me straight back with, "Okay, come on."

I immediately thought about my children and how I could never leave them. They were my life. I changed my mind.

That was when I realized how deeply I was loved. As I fell back to sleep, I was awakened, finding myself on a bridge walking toward a huge industrial city that appeared to be run-down and dilapidated. I kept holding on to the railing of the bridge so as not to fall into the puffy white snowballs that appeared and looked to come in UPS packages. So, I would fall into them but would bounce right back up onto the bridge making it to the other side.

From there, I entered a room and was blown away by all the unique textures of wood that were layers of dimensions roaming the walls, seemingly alive, and breathing sounds of music that I felt were communicating songs inside me. It was a small room, but it had no ceiling above, only songs of words that I danced with as I entered another small room. On top of a beautiful dresser was a small book but as I opened it, I saw every movement of me from a seed inside the womb to my adult being. I was able to see every moment that my body had ever experienced all at once, in a blink of an eye.

I then ventured outside, where a huge and beautiful tree shaded the grass that was alive and full of song just as the walls were inside my room. I dove into the bluest of emerald waters that again fully embraced me in dancing with songs. I was with every soul I ever loved and all those who loved me were in this universe composed of the water. I was in the most incredible atmosphere, where I knew I belonged. Then I woke up.

After I woke up, I realized that I did have a purpose and that I was supposed to be here for my kids. However, most of all I realized how loved I was because everything felt so real in my dream. I felt so accepted in knowing that God loves me so much that he would've got me out of there as I desired. He showed me what I had to look forward to, and it's as if that vision has always been there planted within me that I hold onto knowing that that's my true home where my spirit will go and be for eternity. This is my true home.

*This is how I fight my battles.*

## 15. Forgiveness and Healing

Once again, I find myself on the floor hyperventilating and breathing into a paper bag when I walked away from my marriage. I knew what I had to do. It was my very first brave act of getting up on my feet and walking through a dark, heavy forest toward a small flicker of light shining through the trees. I realized that my eyes were opened wide, looking up and focused directly on the little light. I was beginning to understand that it was my journey and only mine alone and that it would start with me getting up from the floor to my feet and then onto my path, taking my first steps. My hard work was beginning to take root, in me first.

- Step 1 – Forgiving myself.
- Step 2 – Forgiveness to others.
- Step 3 – Healing begins.

When I realized that it was not my dad's fault, my mom's fault, or my husband's fault, I finally began to understand that it was nobody's fault, not even my own. There was nobody to blame for my unhappiness. Especially with me lying there and pissed off at the world for putting me on the floor like that, I had to realize that the world had nothing to do with it. I had to feel all of this to heal all of this.

Forgiving me, so I'm able to forgive you, then the peace comes along with the freedom of healing.

After I got my wake-up call and discovered my path to freedom out of the forest, with my eyes focused on the light above, I was able to leave my unhappiness, releasing all those dark, ugly, vibes of others. They want to remain and stay stuck in their guilt, shame, and blame, believing that's all they deserve. I call them life suckers. They literally will suck the life out of you when you hang out with them.

However, when you cover them with loving-kindness and forgiveness and have your strong boundaries in place, nothing they say or do can get to you.

*This is how I fight my battles.*

### **I Can Forgive Others, But Can I Forgive Myself?**

A question I asked Darla was, "What is it with me if I can forgive everybody, and I mean everybody, but not me, myself?

Why am I having such a hard time forgiving myself?" "I don't know, Pat, you need to ask yourself that question.

Why can't you forgive yourself?"

I've spent hours, turning into days, months and now it's been years, going through this forgiveness process with others. It is some of the hardest work I have done. So many different processes and attempts, such as taking blown-up balloons and writing down with magic marker the names of offenders and the offenses done to me, then I'd have this little let go and release party and watch them fly up, up, and away, disappearing into the sky.

I have written pages of offenses that were made against me with people's names and lengthy paragraphs on how I felt they had wronged me. I then would have a sit-down and personal pretend conversation with each person in telling them how I felt when they hurt me. The conversation would end with me forgiving them, releasing the offense by a check mark, and signing off with my name.

Then I would have a ceremony with a funeral of all these pages of hurts against me. Light a match while watching them burn and turning into ashes and releasing them with total forgiveness. I would then dig a hole and bury them in my backyard.

Although I went through all these drastic measures and felt at that time that I had to for me to move on, it is only now that I am learning to respond with pure forgiveness in love by allowing my SPIRIT to lead. This enables my power to exalt with each breath.

### *Forgiveness is Simply Living in the Moment*

My practice on forgiveness and healing is moment by moment and now takes place in my meditation, prayer, and yoga, in every breath I take.

Back on being busy with the 3 B's – Betrayal, Beauty, and the Beast.

I developed into my physical appearance rather early, which got me in a lot of trouble. In fact, at the age of fourteen, I once caused a car collision just walking to the mall in my shorts and tube top.

An older man was slowly and carefully backing out of his driveway when a convertible with four younger guys were all flirting and looking at me driving right into the poor old man's car.

Girls and women hate me, and some still do.

I would be hanging out with my girlfriend in a place that we shouldn't be at the age of sixteen and notice a girl sitting next to her boyfriend staring at me giving me dirty looks or an evil eye.

I would try to ignore it, but I could just feel the tension of bad energy in feeling the fiery darts coming at me. Sure enough, she would end up coming up to me or grabbing me. I would merely be walking by going to the bathroom and get attacked by a mean girl trying to fight me. Thank God, I was never alone and would always have a friend there to back me up.

So that's why the majority of my friends were guys, and there were always plenty surrounding me, especially in college.

When I first met Darla, I was in school full time and a single mother living in a nice apartment complex. My baby girl was safely kept on the first floor at the babysitters with Ms. Faye.

### *College for Me, I Needed Help!*

I had a science project that was due, and all my friends were all about helping me get it done. They were my buddies and loved hanging out with me so they would come over to my place, never empty-handed, maybe bringing a gallon of milk or diapers or supplies for my science project.

So, I guess I had a bad reputation because of the jealous girls fearing I would steal their boyfriends; they'd gossip, making up bad rumors and calling me a skanky, little ho.

Being single in college and having a baby was very difficult for me. I struggled, but I guess the forgiveness and healing were helping me get through it, to take care of my baby.

### *How We Met*

Before we knew each other as friends, one Friday night, Darla was visiting her married friends, my neighbor down the hall, and her friend Bob said, "Let's go to Pat's place."

Darla said, "No. I don't want to go there. I don't want to go to her place. She's a bad person."

However, Bob talked her into it, and she came dressed in a robe borrowed from his wife. We finally met at the entry to my place. She ended up staying for three days.

We just talked about this recently on the phone, about how when she walked in the door there were maybe a half a dozen guys everywhere, one asleep on the couch, two around my kitchen table, another playing his guitar, one behind my studio desk and the remainder in the middle of my living room floor doing my science project.

Darla and I, for the life of us, couldn't remember what my school project was. I think it was a spaceless chair we created out of cardboard. Most of my guy friends were nerds, incredibly smart, and were always helping me because of my dyslexia that I never professed to have.

Darla said it was magical and mystical when she walked into my world. I didn't own a television, only conversation took up space in my place, for I was a full-time mother first and fulltime college student, plus working for Social Services as a driver as I could bring my baby girl with me. I was also modeling, and my daughter and I made a video about the abuse that Social Services used in their training.

## *My New Family Tribe, The Brede Bunch*

Darla and I became best friends on that weekend. Her parents became my parents and Tatum's grandparents as we were so far away from mine.

I had another neighbor on my floor that Darla knew and who hated my guts. She thought I wanted her pathetic looking boyfriend and wanted to start a fight when she knocked at my door. I pressed the button to buzz her in. Much to her surprise, Darla opened my door, gave her a stern look, and asked flatly, "What do you want?"

Darla stands five-foot-nine and has a strong and self-assured presence. We both enjoyed watching her run away. She never bothered me again.

Another jealous girl who lived on the second floor had spread many made-up lies, saying that I was abusing my baby girl and had even reported me to Social Services. She didn't realize I worked closely with them in that very same department. Of course, they knew the truth and made me aware. I was so upset when I found out that I went up to face her and give her a piece of my mind.

### *Brave and Stupid Me*

She had left her husband and son to ride off with a dude in a seedy gang. They were all on their bikes in the parking lot when I walked up to her as they formed a big circle with us in the middle. Then out of nowhere, pops out of the crowd, my friend, Gary, who snatched me quickly into his arms and escaped with me in the car that he'd left running nearby.

I know he saved my life because she probably would've killed me.

Forgiveness is something I practice this day every time I have a major setback with somebody. I always pray and forgive them soon after. I feel that's the only way I could ever heal. I need to forgive instantly and move on so the hurt could not take hold and affect me in my body, mind, and emotions.

### *From Mean Girls to Mean Old Ladies*

This drama of jealousy with mean-ass girls on my ass has been a life-long ordeal for me, and still, it goes on. It has never stopped; not even when I was married. It got worse.

I was too busy to let jealousy drama bother me; except on one occasion when we had just moved into an incredibly beautiful home.

I'd always go all-out in decorating for the holidays. I had joined the neighborhood ladies' book club, and they were organizing a Christmas tree toast at a handful of the homes, and mine was one. I was so excited about preparing with buying specialty wines and having my house ready for the celebration. Within just thirty minutes of my portion of hosting for the event, they said that they didn't need my home, so I was out.

I cried for days, and my husband again was shocked at the way the women behaved. However, I had my true and amazing lifetime girlfriends that I write about in all my stories, and that is more than enough.

Even now, as I am working in the Castle, there are some toxic stares in the lunchroom or the passing glances in the halls now and then. I keep being me and being busy in not allowing their fear to contaminate my space.

It's not as bad as it is sad because I have been dealing with this practically my whole life and am used to it. I don't know these ladies and don't have any desire to get to know them if they are going to gossip and talk behind others' backs.

### *Trust*

The saddest form of betrayal is when it comes from a close friend who for years you've bonded with and trusted. When I was going through my divorce, I went on a cruise with a longtime trusted friend. Even in knowing all that I was going through, she was reporting all the information back to my ex.

We were roommates on the ship. In the middle of the night, I had a nightmare, and as I sat straight up in the bed, I put my hand out in front of her, and I said, "Stop! No, get away from me! Why? Because you are evil."

This is exactly what I spoke out loud because she told me what I had said so that I could write it down in my journal. It was soon after returning from the cruise that my ex told me all I had done. My friend and I both knew then why I had spoken out those words in my sleep.

To me, I believe that was my SPIRIT speaking out through me to a beast that had taken over my friend. I had to release many balloons and burn many papers from that experience. Soon after, I had another longtime friend pretty much betray me in the same manner.

It's beautiful now that I may honestly write that nothing like those two betrayals from close friends has happened to me since.

We're human beings, and when our bodies take on the stress of anger, resentment, and unforgiveness, we are denying our force of SPIRIT the space to lead the way.

The wicked beast will rule.

However, who has time for that?

*This is how I fight my battles.*

## 16. Removing My Mask

Yikes, I do admit that I tend to feel the need to wear my mask. I guess what I mean here is that I've spent my whole life trying to be normal like everybody else where I wore a mask and just recently took it off by coming to grips with my learning disability and all the other stuff that's been covered up. I know I'm going to make mistakes and I'm human and it's just something I must be aware.

However, when I became aware of my need to wear it, I now know firsthand it is not always easy to remove it. Especially when I've been wearing it for practically my whole life. It is difficult to look at yourself and be deeply honest about what you find inside. However, the only way for you to start walking a better path is to face up to your truths. Yes, it takes courage to ask yourself the hard questions.

- Am I at peace?
- Am I experiencing the love I desire in my life?
- Am I honoring my own soul?

There were times when I was with my Aussie boyfriend and he would tap on my chest and say "Patricia, I want what's in here.

I want this." Tap, tap, tap! "What's in here."

I was so dazed and confused, wondering what he was talking about. Then his next question was even more difficult for me to answer, "Patricia, what do you want?"

That one hit a nerve because I honestly could not answer it; why? I honestly did not know. It frustrated me to no end. This was indeed the very beginning of me allowing love in, just for me. I got an authentic taste, and I wanted more.

I cannot recall a time in my life when any lover ever sought out my soul, caring enough to want to share and know me that deeply.

### *When Being Yourself is Enough for Yourself*

Relationships can teach you so much when you're willing to receive love and listen. After all, who can know you better sometimes than your significant other? The key here is to master that art from within. No love or another human being can do that for you. So how selfish would it be to expect your most loving companion, your mate, to save you? I must continue every day now to remember to remove my mask for only I can do so. I'm not perfect but I do try to notice now when I'm beginning to cover up my true self. I do this by asking myself the hard questions and facing up to my truth within. Everyone suffers. There are no perfect people. I choose to be and come from a place of peace; a decision made from my inner self.

Worrying for me is merely walking on eggshells while carrying a tray full of snacks, trying to deliver everyone's needs – what I think they're needing; but my own needs? Hmm, I didn't see it coming.

I ask myself, "What do I want and need, Patricia Ann?" I'm still my work in progress.

I don't expect anything from anyone, including me. So, when I am real, walking in the fruits of the spirit, my beautiful life experiences fabulous results; results I could never even begin to imagine.

*This is how I fight my battles.*

I will now do a recap in how I wear my mask, being in:

### *Love*

Hate is a place where I will admit to having dwelled much too often. Even amidst such chaos, I had no clue at the time that I was in a prison of my own making. I was embroiled in, and far too preoccupied with, operating from the wounds of my past. At the time, this was what I knew, and it felt like my comfort/safe zone.

I wore my mask of love especially when I was married, getting my husband to buy me bigger houses, bigger diamonds and name brand purses that were bigger than what Carrie's closet could hold in the *Sex and the City* movie.

I know I come off as being the best, most supportive, goody two-shoes. But back then I had more shoes than Imelda Marcos, and I was very materialistic. In fact, I am ashamed to admit that I wore that mask throughout our marriage.

I am still working through this as I sometimes tend to make a stupid purchase of four-hundred-dollar designer sunglasses, will get pissed at myself, but then I take some deep breaths and return them.

I may wear this love mask only occasionally now, but I don't keep it on for long as I am now aware, and I remove it. I also am aware that taking care of my BODY in my everyday rituals, such as taking my vitamins, brushing my teeth, getting plenty of rest are key factors for self-love maintenance.

Breathing in my daily practice of meditation and yoga, with prayer at night and when I wake up, are all part of the maintenance. I pray over myself and loved ones first thing in the morning as I wait on my first and only cup of coffee for the day.

I have been secretly praying/talking to God my entire life. Now as an ADULT, I cannot ever think back to a time when even as a CHILD I haven't done so. These talks are alive, natural, and the purest form of foundational make-up that I wear on my soul.

Believing and knowing that my SPIRIT leads, and I am present as one in *My Fight Club Within* allows me to operate from the truth that love will keep us together!

I am so excited to be going to see my kids over Easter in 2019 to witness my grandson being born.

Pure love for me is spending quality time with my kids. There is no place I'd rather be than hanging out with them. I miss them!

## *Joy*

Sorrow rolls into shock and awakens my inner being with a gut-jerk reaction inside my knotted throat as my belly begins to ache. Again, the seats are taken in each corner of the boxing ring within my being. Dark clouds now blanketing over those beautiful rays of sunshine while the soft waves are now crashing thunder within.

I guess I've kept this Joy Mask permanently planted on my face until just recently when I wrote chapter eleven on Secrets.

It was the most excruciating and hardest thing I've ever done opening my heart totally to the outside world.

My throat has begun to knot up now as I type these words. However, it's not as bad as it was just recently in the past few days. I feel that I was holding onto my inner CHILD in keeping my secret.

The ADULT in me thinks back on all the years that have gone by when I would sit reserved and in total denial, but that hidden lump in my throat and sick belly (BODY) would be active with the subject matter of abortion.

I will continue in being faithful walking in love for myself with forgiveness and gentle kindness of which I am so deserving of in my ongoing healing process.

I know now the best is yet to come with each breath I take. I am SPIRIT-led, walking in freedom, being my true, authentic self.

There is no greater joy than the sound of laughter coming from the lips of all my grandbabies. I continue to watch all our self-made videos full of laughter, music, and dance in my everyday rituals of love.

## *Peace*

Anxiety can come over me without warning, the very moment I start worrying and thinking about my future or dwelling over my past. Fear can set in quickly, stealing my peace with worries such as, "Will I have enough money? Why didn't I tell him how I was feeling?"

Grrr... here comes that tell-tale clearing of the throat and then down to my unsettled tummy. All the while, my SPIRIT is yearning for a group hug and the opportunity to illuminate the way out of this silly nonsense.

Yikes, the Peace Mask is what I learned to wear early on to survive my dysfunctional CHILDhood. I had no other choice. Raz, my brilliant Hoffman teacher, very patiently explained how I was still stuck in the emotionally immature manner of how I was treated in my past relationships.

I would avoid conflict at all costs. I would not subject my BODY to any form of mature conversation that is so necessary to have in a healthy relationship.

I get it now, and it's tough to be a grown-up. Facing myself now in the mirror and seeing myself naked and raw, I am not that Patsy. Fuck no! I am smart, savvy, witty and brave. I am here in my bed, as I write

*My Fight Club Within.* Yes, this is me celebrating and still on my honeymoon. I am living the scene in another one of my favorite movies, Under the Tuscan Sun. The lead character was in her bed after the big storm and best sex ever with her hot lover and just like her; I still got it!

I, not acting but being an ADULT, am certain and totally confident in announcing that, yes, I have now had my seventh date with Good Man. I had my guy over for dinner and a movie at my place. We are having mature conversations, and he understands that I am still raw and healing from my breakup, so we are taking it slow.

My top priority is remaining true and patient with my growing up and catching up to myself with my SPIRIT leading me in love every breath of the way.

I now am talking the talk and walking the walk on such a beautiful, blissful level with myself.

Peace begins within.

> *I love people who make me laugh. I honestly think it's the thing I like most, to laugh. It cures a multitude of ills. It's probably the most important thing in a person. ~Audrey Hepburn*

### *Patience*

Frustration laid heavy on my shoulders shortly after moving to the beach and after many attempts of working hard at creating my dreams and making them come true. My friends and family from whom I moved far away thought at first, I was crazy to leave. However, all I kept imagining was my atmosphere where the sea, earth, and sky connect, surrounded by beauty with my toes in the sand, watching sweet nature jumping up out of the water under a sky full of breathtaking sunrises and sunsets. However, sadly, within the first couple of days of living by the sea, I was taken with the panic and frustration of being without all my city conveniences such as Whole Foods, Spouts, Discount Tires, sushi restaurants, and even friends in my new area. I knew no one.

I was so impatient and frustrated that I wasn't enjoying being present in living and experiencing my dream. So, my friends and family went from telling me how crazy I was to "how brave are you to make such a big move! Do you realize that there are very few people that partake in a lifetime that will never do such a thing? And look at you girl, you are doing it! Living your dream! You are in paradise."

I used to make my life so much more complicated than it is merely, especially wearing my Patience Mask, jumping to crazy and mindless ADULT ego conclusions. The more I'd try to cover up endless clusterfucks, not even mine, the worse it got. I felt others, and their drama needed my full attention.

My car situation is a good example. I had no patience for their lack of service but felt I had the answers in judging how they needed to run their business. I, of course, took on their drama in trying to fix and fit them perfectly into my universe of a perfect atmosphere.

Today, a remarkable change took place not only in just me but in the once dreaded dealership I wanted to avoid like the plague. They've given me the best service in fixing my key matter, replaced my brakes at cost, and brought me a brand-new car that I drove, "Not really because I walked everywhere," for almost two weeks.

Going through the growing pains of my CHILDish ways, and their issues as well, caused all our BODY's unneeded stress. When I gave up and surrendered to my SPIRIT, it was able to release much favor on me and out to the universe.

I have new brakes now, and my new car dealership is where I'll take my happy car for all its needs. I love how simple and wonderfully

*My Fight Club Within* works for me, and I adore its remarkable force, watching its energy illuminate others.

### *Kindness*

Meanness to myself occurs when I absorb the emotions of others, usually beginning in my stomach. I call them my dark uglies. I stew in my endless head drama chattering along, endlessly recirculating through each pain in some effort to make it better. After all, I know the way and my head insists I can think myself into the solution. Shh, shh, now be quiet, Ms. Ego. Hmmm, as I am writing this book for me, first, and you, I am learning to set boundaries by listening to my gut. After all, they say the stomach is our second brain that can sense surrounding information, an energy that our eyes cannot see.

When there's no self-respect or healthy boundaries how can I get respect from others?

This has been my most used Mask in being too overly kind to others. This one caused me to lose myself totally.

Having my good friend and accountability partner, Darla, my supportive, awesome banker friend, Kenny, my therapist, Michelle, my yoga instructor, contributing editor, and beautiful friend, Liz, and my business advisor, PR and web designer, brilliantly minded friend, Jim, has been a support of grand portion. This is my unseen heavenly team choir that has been singing throughout my words from all these pages of *My Fight Club Within*.

Singing our praises in one accord of their belief is captured and played out as the bottom line on every page of *My Fight Club Within*.

That bottom line is most important.

*This is how I fight my battles.*

Having genuine, authentic, and healthy relationships is key. These five beautiful souls had seen and met the real me even before I did.

I had no clue or idea that all along it wasn't my dead first boyfriend, grandparents, baby, or ex that I was in mourning for and missing in my life.

It was me.

I was missing me.

It is a world like no other when you discover LOVE, meeting, and laying eyes upon oneself for the first time. I see through and into the very center of my pupil that radiates a glow of multiple one-of-a-kind colors from my soul's portal. It is there where my SPIRIT dwells and awaits my call to come and kick some ass out of my Paradise.

## *Goodness*

Selfishness is giving love to get love. However, oh, how I quickly discovered it only leaves me empty and never satisfied. This causes constant havoc on my BODY while at the same time imprisoning me inside my head. Currently my head is no friendly place to be now the isolated boxing ring with mindless CHILDhood tantrums warring with my fearful ADULT ego, refusing to allow my true SPIRIT to free me. BODY is currently dazed and confused, screaming out with pain, "Please stop your fighting!"

Hmmm, I know this has been one of the hardest masks to remove, and I'm sure, if I were in Hollywood at the Academy Awards, I would win the Oscar for my acting role as Ms. Goody Two-Shoes.

No more acting for me in wearing the Goodness Mask, as I have removed it from my face for goodness sake.

I have always been a seeker of honesty and believing that everybody felt the same way. I never could understand or imagine why on earth people would go through all that trouble in making up stories when the truth is so much easier to remember.

Three of my favorite things in life that are often free are conversation, music, and dance. I have been attending concerts, even partying backstage with some of the most famous bands, throughout my life. Those were amazing times, but I don't want to take up space in *My Fight Club Within* in bragging. After all, the most amazing concerts I attended involved taking my kids along to off-the-beaten-path places like old high school auditoriums. We saw Mercy Me and Amy Grant in places just like that in Texas. I would be holding my daughter's hand, and my other would be pushing the double stroller with my boys comfortably enjoying their gas station treats that I bought on the way to the concert.

Just recently before I made my move to Paradise, I saw the Mercy Me movie entitled *I Can Only Imagine*. It was as if I walked back in time. Same stories, only our dads were not alcoholics, so the only excuse was pure downright anger in lashing out at us.

The movie is about growing up in Greenville, Texas. Bart Millard has a rough childhood, but when his abusive father becomes ill, he mends his relationship with his dad with the help of faith and music.

I feel we are spiritually connected as to how we were able to love and forgive our fathers. How beautiful his life story is playing out as is mine as I have been opening my heart and relinquishing my all to our HOLY SPIRIT.

### *I Can Only Imagine. Faithfulness*

There is no mask to be worn in covering up faithfulness because I believe.

This is a repeat of chapter seven as I may have lost myself, but I have always kept my faith in my God.

Faithfulness is being true to myself as I remind myself daily of that beautiful commitment and the vow I made to myself. Faithfulness always goes hand-in-hand with accountability. I hold myself accountable by investing in myself.

Recently I attended the most incredible life-changing program called the *Hoffman Process*. These were the best ten days of my entire life and by far, one of the most significant investments that I have ever gifted to myself. Selling my diamond earrings and exchanging that energy for this process delivered lifechanging results for me.

Even operating to the best of my ability, I have learned to ask for help. I get therapy and seek out assistance when I feel stuck inside a boxing round too long. It's a beautiful gift to be faithful, accountable and true-to-self by receiving help when I need it. Outstanding results can then occur, getting me back on track, resulting in again walking in faith with love to myself and others. I committed to myself in the first chapter of this book, and I'm holding true and keeping my vows.

The true manifestation of my SPIRIT allows for walking and dancing with so much love, joy, peace, patience, kindness, and goodness while cherishing every moment. Disregard of these truths can stop me in my tracks with a sudden, dark, and ugly string of lies that pops into my head. "I'm just not enough. I don't deserve this. I made a foolish mistake in marrying me."

"Oh, Patricia Ann, remember that faithful vow I made to you?" I lovingly remind myself.

When I was pregnant, I enjoyed writing poetry and singing to my babies. So, from a very young age we would sing and create songs, joining in our own flavor of words together in a loving expression of harmony.

I have just recently begun to sing again.

A new song.

Eight is a beautiful number and come Thanksgiving 2019, I will have eight children in all (three children and five grandchildren) with my grandbaby boy's arrival. I am so blown away by how amazingly blessed that I am to have these beautiful, healthy children. I am astonished by how they came from my parents and me, sharing all our features and likeness. The phrase that automatically comes out of those who meet us is, "Oh my God, you have wonderful and beautiful children."

## *Gentleness*

When my mom was suffering from Alzheimer's, she forgot everybody; her husband, son, sister, grandchildren, and friends – everybody but me. It was so bizarre because she knew me precisely as I was, and we would talk every single day on the phone. The hardest thing for me is that I felt her pain. However, being with her when she died was the most beautiful experience of our life together as mother and daughter. I allowed my SPIRIT to lead me, and it was there so very present with us.

I know that I lived a large part of my life, keeping a promise to myself to not be like my mother. I have taken that Mask off, and I think about my mother and the gentle and loving heart that she has so beautifully passed on to me.

Every day as I look back at my reflection in the mirror, and I see my mother's deep and glowing hazel eyes in mine. As I brush my long, thick, and beautiful hair I see my mother and how she always took care of her long hair in her younger years. Then she went short and permed, and I'm sorry, but hell no with all that. When I go all out in planning and preparation for birthdays, holidays, meals, extra specially prepared for my loved ones, I think of her. Every day as I watch and listen to the birds sing, I think of how much my mom loved nature and all the exotic birds she had and had me buy. I smile about how she can't pronounce some of her words, mine are different too, such as fajitas, she would call them, "va-chea-das." My boys would laugh and say, "vaginas." My word is, and my boys will ask me to say it – sandwiches; I say, "san-wedges." I hear my daughter laugh the very same laugh as my mom's and my own.

I watch her move her hands; they too look just like Mom's.

I am just like my mom.

I am me embracing all her unique and beautiful qualities that I know my dad had once found and fallen in love. It is that same beautiful love that I embrace, passing it down to my beautiful and amazing children. They know where they came from and how they are in some ways just like me.

It is 5 a.m. and I am having my coffee in bed as I do most of my writing on my laptop desk here in the early morning. I am finishing up this chapter as I will print it out then tuck it in my yoga pants as I will deliver it over to Liz at 9:00 a.m. before yoga begins on the beach.

*My Fight Club Within* is the drug that has and continues to affect me deeply. In conversation with my friend Darla recently, I had such a revelation of hard truth in my findings that have surfaced from within. I didn't realize how sad I've been; the direct effects manifested as harsh behavior with the grief of missing me. My sad mask has been mostly worn alone, just with me.

I am wearing it now as I am typing out these thoughts of my ADULT ego, CHILD, and BODY. Not including my SPIRIT to release this pain, it continues to thicken.

However, as I am now aware of facing and feeling my painful brokenness, my SPIRIT is still at work and in control. I am blown away by how this shit I am writing really works.

Recently, I watched the movie *Why Him*. It's absolutely hilarious, starring James Franco and Bryan Cranston. Talk about a free and fun SPIRIT-led character.

*Why Him* is all about a dad who learns that his beautiful and smart daughter is dating his biggest nightmare, a socially awkward guy who seems not to have a lot going for him, even worse, the dad learns the boyfriend is about to propose.

After explaining to Darla in our phone conversation about my newfound discovery of losing, missing, and now finding me, she said, "Let me go sit down for this."

I listened to her as she gave her impression of how she too, has been missing me. She began to share with me all the times in my life when I indeed had my shit together. That being when after going through my first divorce, she first met me and my three-month-old baby girl. Then after my last separation and divorce when I became healthy by journaling and becoming a fitness and nutrition guru.

She went on to say I was the strongest yet happiest and content, fun-loving friend that had changed into a frustrated and pissed off at the world friend. She went on to explain that when I moved to Paradise, I had such high expectations as to having everything set up in place to fulfill my needs. I replied, "Now that I am aware that I have been acting as pretty much a twelve-year-old brat, have I grown up any in these past two days?"

When I finally extended my inner self out to the universe, I was able to receive, embrace and engage, experiencing that oh so wonderfully fabulous moment and that love that is right there within my reach.

My transformation began taking form with these three simple steps:

Step 1. Awareness – if I feel

Step 2. Action – I can heal

Step 3. Allow – and be real

*This is how I fight my battles.*

## **Self-Control**

Indulgence is when my boundaries are poor and weak. I then run away to escape. This continues with me getting stuck in those negative emotions of hate, sorrow, anxiety, frustration, meanness, selfishness, disregard, and harshness all sticking in my body, making me ill.

I have been running from the start. I can still hear those words spoken regularly by my dad, "Patsy, walk, stop running." I also remember how I wore out my tennis shoes with my dad complaining of having to buy me monthly shoes because I would wear holes in them.

As my conversation carried on with Darla, I referred to how I handled my car situation. I asked, "How could I have handled it differently, still having the same conversations that needed to be spoken, for the growth of the dealership and mature emotional growth with me?"

Darla replied, "Very simple. You have no control over other people. You only have control over you."

I must learn how to remove my expectations of others and myself.

"I'm fucked. How do I do this?" is my immediate gut (BODY) and ADULT ego reaction.

However, you know what, I do know how to do this!

It is navigated gracefully when I am accepting of the other person in being who they are. It's love, when I let you be you, and you let me be me. Would you maybe agree with me that this sweet CHILD of mine is growing up? I have been practicing this; at least I was when I had a boyfriend. So now I am aware.

Relaxing for me is key. It was so easy to relax when I was physically in the arms of my boyfriend. Learning how to love me alone in the arms of my SPIRIT is heaven now.

It is now 7:45 a.m. and I will get up and print out these pages to begin my therapy with sweet Liz as I breathe in her amazingly beautiful words of wisdom as she delivers in song what my SPIRIT needs.

My spiritual emotions of love, joy, peace, patience, kindness, gentleness, and self-control cover all of me, inside and out, with light.

Yes, the light is what sets me free, and my wedding reception is the place to be for me. That's where there are dancing and singing and moving to the grooving.

My race is over, and I am a winner. I am happy, settled and at home here in Paradise.

*This is how I fight my battles.*

## 17. Change

*Galatians 5:22-23 – "But the fruit of the Spirit is love, joy, peace, longsuffering, gentleness, goodness, faith, meekness, temperance: against such there is no law."*

When I was going into the third grade, I began attending parochial school. My dad and I attended mass every time the church doors were open. We were on time every time as I was under the total control and beat of my dad.

### Religion

I was studying for my spelling test with the help of my nanny, and I couldn't spell the word religion. My dad was nearby and overheard me getting it wrong. He then grabbed a board and proceeded to beat me until the nanny silently lipped out, "R—e—l—i—g—i—o—n."

That was one of the very pivotal moments that marked my discovery of my genuine personal relationship with God, and my faith began as the root of my means of survival in this world. I learned how to truly talk with God one-on-one that day.

I pray, and I believe.

It is not my purpose by any shape or form to take up any space on these pages going back into the dark unknown to trigger the pain of childhood history or toxic or abusive relationships we've had, or are still in, or any self-guilt, blame, or shame on ourselves or others. My sole desire is to simply share myself and how I fight my battles.

By sharing the dark story above about my dad is to reveal that I have no ill feelings, anger, or unforgiveness toward him or any human being for that matter. However, I will express that there is just one word that I honestly detest and is repulsive to me. Yes, that word is religion. This is me in accepting my true feelings for a dislike of a word. In fact, it doesn't even have anything to do with my dad beating me because I didn't know it. I do not like the definition and meaning of it. I am not affiliated with any religious beliefs.

## *My Foundational Steps for Change*

1) **Love** – You must first love yourself. Doing so will bring about the healthy results you're wanting.

2) **Joy** – Spending time with others, walking, laughing, and smiling is key. Having a generous heart is how you will experience a joyful spirit.

3) **Peace** – Being alone in nature looking at the trees, water, and animals will wrap you in perfect peace.

4) **Patience** – Deep breathing, journaling, and smiling a lot are some of the ways to practice patience with yourself and others.

5) **Kindness** – Show kindness to yourself and others. This creates a healthy environment within you and around you.

6) **Goodness** – Be good to yourself and others. Doing so brings goodness back to you. This, too, creates a healthy and nurturing environment for you and others.

7) **Faithfulness** – Believe in yourself and believe that you will focus on and move forward with the good things you are accomplishing. Have faith in what your heart is telling you to be, to do, and to have.

8) **Gentleness** – Gentleness with yourself is key, for it is the only way you can give gentleness to others.

9) **Self-control** – Setting appropriate boundaries in your life turns overindulgence and excess into healthy choices that help produce the life changes that you want.

## *Practicing Mindfulness Versus Negativity*

When your thoughts become negative the opposite of the nine fruits listed above, you fill your soul with useless things:

1) Hate

2) Sorrow

3) Anxiety

4) Frustration

5) Meanness

6) Selfishness

7) Disregard

8) Harshness

9) Indulgence

You must recognize these for how destructive they are. Whatever you do, do not dwell on these, or stay here. You must detach immediately.

Change is such a small six-letter word, but we're faced with it every single moment of every single day. Not one human being ever stays the same; we are all constantly changing.

Every day there's a constant change happening in our universe, and with me, I depleted my desires, needs, and in the wake of everybody else's.

I've spent the majority of my life working diligently on changing everything around me. I always thought, "Oh, if only I had a different mom, or if only I had a different dad, or if only I had a different husband, or if only I could change my kids."

I'd spend hours moving my furniture around every other month, thinking that if only I beautify my atmosphere, I would feel more complete. Then, to add more to my heap of my "if only's," I would take on the responsibilities of everyone else's "if only." To name a few, if only I had worn a different outfit, we had a different president, I was thirty pounds lighter, I had a thicker head of hair, etc., etc., etc…

All my drama, your drama, and the world's drama were suffocating my true self. With giving all my space and energy to the drama, it is easy to understand why I was so overwhelmed, frustrated, and pissed at my boyfriend for asking that one small question, "What do you want?" Followed by his tap, tap, tap on my heart while saying, "I want what's in here."

### *Even Though I Felt I was Totally Committed to Him in Love, Was I Committed to Myself?*

If we welcome and embrace our inner true wants and desires by developing a healthy daily practice by which we commit to loving ourselves, not others, first, I believe we can change the world. However, it starts individually within ourselves, first, one person at a time.

My heart's desire is to extend my story, reaching out to every soul community, schools, and the heart of our world, helping to teach our children at a young age how to fight their battles. This is very close to my heart because I was one of those young students sitting in geography class doodling pictures, bored out of my mind, struggling to bring home a C.

What if I could've been sitting in a classroom and learning about me and how to be my authentic self? Developing the understanding that I have beautiful gifts to offer that are not like everybody else's? Nourishing acceptance of the truth that we are all so uniquely different human beings that are not perfect and never have to be? That being consumed by our future career and how much money we'll make and mastering pretending to be someone we are not to bring home that A is unnecessary? Discovering my uniqueness instead of just my weaknesses of feeling like a failure?

It was ingrained early on by my teacher and my grades that I didn't measure up. The weak presentation of my sweet, kind, loving self was not acceptable to what the teacher expected of me. My education in a costly private school taught me absolutely nothing. At least not in geography. It wasn't until just recently when I traveled the world with my Aussie boyfriend that I realized that I am a work in progress and I'll never know everything, especially with my lack of direction when I tend to immediately walk in the opposite direction! I have, however, discovered an epic love now for geography and about our natural world that we are all so brilliantly, beautiful, and uniquely designed to be extraordinary spiritual beings having a human experience!

Goodbyes have always been hard for me. Although this is my very first book and I am about to end it, I feel compelled to write that this may be just the beginning of a tap, tap, tap on your heart or for somebody you love out there in the universe who needs this.

As the excitement of concluding this book builds within my heart, it brings me full circle to the excitement I recall within the heart of a good friend of mine, Debby. In the very beginning of this book journey, I was sharing with her some of what I had just started writing. I couldn't even get through the first two paragraphs of my introduction without her bawling her eyes out and insisting that I get this published ASAP because she will read it over and over again. I am still smiling inside with so much love, joy, peace, patience, kindness, goodness, faithfulness, gentleness, and self-control. What a privilege and honor it has been here with you in *My Fight Club Within*.

Love and peace out to you, my friend, out there in our wonderful universe; love that is always within our heavenly, magical, and mystical reach.

*This is how I fight my battles.*

# Epilogue

My fight club within (self-love) has always dwelled deep inside me. I feel we all start created in love regardless of how our parents feel or felt about each other in our hour of conception.

Every human being is unique and comes from a one-of-a-kind seed, and one-of-a-kind and unique set of seeded parents. Regardless of who they are or have become, some may be total dicks or the opposite, living like Mother Theresa. One fact that cannot be ignored and must be acknowledged is that the seed was formed, making a baby, and that baby is you.

There is a MAJOR difference in you being you and me being me.

If I dare say or write this, I became obsessed with love in maybe wanting too much, so much that my heart has been overflowing and bursting out since the moment I felt my baby girl inside me.

I smothered my kids with love and affection and still do but in a healthy measure.

Yes, from observing my parents' good qualities, those of Ms. Sue and Mr. Howard, my dad's next-door neighbors, Carl and Mary (my mom's next-door neighbors), and Lillian and Whitey, neighbors across the street from my mom, I was able to offer the many facets of pure love to my children.

So, I had three happily married couples as my surrogate parents with sixteen kids between them that were my playmates and siblings. I had more love and attention constantly pouring out onto me than my own parents, Fred and Vera, could ever dare compete with.

My dad, Fred, was the only child from his wealthy Catholic dad (also Fred) migrating from Germany with his Jewish wife, Anna.

My mom, Vera, was the youngest child of seven. Her poor dad migrated from France with her mom, who was Cherokee, Irish, and Canadian. She died at the age of twenty-eight when my mom was two.

Having four sets of parents, with all their uniquely flawed characteristics, taught me so much about the importance of valuing myself. I learned from them how to be a best friend, wife, daughter, and mother. That's how I raised my kids, enforcing all their beautiful values and good manners and respect for themselves and others.

This is a good thing that I want to highlight here in *My Fight Club Within*. If anyone of you out there were to have the privilege of meeting any of my kids, you would have the pleasure of experiencing extremely intuitive, intelligent, and caring human beings.

*My Fight Club Within* has been a work of pure love and bliss that I had been pouring out onto others more so than onto myself.

I finally "get" it or better yet, "get" me.

My astrological sun sign is Libra, the scales. It is very important and necessary for me to have everyone and everything in its place. Balance and structure are key in getting me through my dyslexia in everything I do.

I have learned how to finally be alone with myself by fighting my ongoing battles – battles I have very much enjoyed sharing with you through words written in love and awareness expressed throughout these pages.

Facing my truth and awareness, my guilt and shame, from the secrets buried deep within, which by the way were rooted in love and understanding all along, I acted out in destructive patterns such as running away and avoiding important adult decisions which were a necessary process in stepping into real freedom. I was stuck way too often, even when I was in a healthy, loving relationship and felt my life was beautiful and in perfect balance, the truth lingered – a truth I have finally accepted.

*My Fight Club Within* has been the organic work of the step-by-step progress in the opening of my heart, which has produced outstanding and miraculous results as these once dry bones inside now contain and exude my ocean of love. I am still a work in progress and, as I have reiterated all through this book, we are humans, nobody is perfect, and we will continue to discover life, especially when making our very own perfect mistakes.

Writing this book in these past ten months has been my longest and hardest walk (fight). It has, however, altogether been the fight that has turned into the peaceful walk I have so needed to become me.

My journey with *My Fight Club Within* began ten years ago with my wake-up call, "Patricia Ann, it is time for you to wake up now. Patricia Ann, it is time for you to wake up now."

The hard work had begun with a lot of deep, deep soul digging, removing layer by layer the toxicity that was weighing me down. I was numb and only existing through my masked BODY and the shell of a pretend ADULT ego in Pat-world. The first step was awareness, which took place immediately upon my wake-up call. I had to take the necessary steps of going into my CHILD fantasy fairytale directly into the woods, keeping my eye on that small flicker of light (SPIRIT) for my truth and reality.

I had to go into my fairytale to come out. Yes, I jumped down into many rabbit holes in facing some of my greatest fears. I experienced more adventures that I learned to love and had deep and hidden desires for but had no idea of what I truly wanted. My hidden desires and dreams have all come alive and true, and my nightmare of loneliness has ended.

Yes, *My Fight Club Within* has a happily-ever-after ending to my fairytale-come-true. This is my true conception of endless love (SPIRIT) where my inner beauty resides in and radiates from deep within me, connecting us by that same kind of deep and true inner beauty that is rooted and grounded in you. This love is grounded within the soil, connecting our steps in this vast universe, and finding one another in the epic air we all breathe.

Traveling throughout the world in each little town, village, city, and state with my Aussie boyfriend hand-in-hand with me every step of the way, we met many extraordinarily beautiful people that would sit down with us and share their personal stories. I'd picture these people as fitting into my sixteen siblings and us dwelling in as neighbors maybe even living next door or across the street in one big, lovely community.

At the time, I couldn't conceive just how much depth, width, and height my heart could consume inside my being while living out my truest heart's desires.

As I will continue my path with my heart wide open, on my journey, being led by my SPIRIT; there is no place to escape my love. Please allow me to introduce myself. Patricia Ann.

*This is how I fight my battles.*

How the best brainstorming sessions end…

DON'T FORGET THE WORKBOOK!

# THIS IS HOW I FIGHT MY BATTLES WORKBOOK

*MY FIGHT CLUB WITHIN*

**AVAILABLE**

Amazon, Barnes & Noble, IngramSpark,
and other online retailers

## Get in Touch

www.patriciasimonwriter.com

www.ingramcontent.com/pod-product-compliance
Lightning Source LLC
Chambersburg PA
CBHW071352290426
44108CB00014B/1509